W9-AOV-227

The Shadow of Ulysses

The Shadow of Ulysses

Public Intellectual Exchange across the U.S.–Mexico Border

José Antonio Aguilar Rivera

Foreword by Russell Jacoby

Translated by Rose Hocker
and Emiliano Corral

LEXINGTON BOOKS
Lanham • Boulder • New York • Oxford

LEXINGTON BOOKS

Published in the United States of America
by Lexington Books
4720 Boston Way, Lanham, Maryland 20706

12 Hid's Copse Road
Cumnor Hill, Oxford OX2 9JJ, England

Translation copyright © 2000 by Lexington Books
Copyright © 1998 by Centro de Investigación y Docencia Económicas.
Originally published under the title *La sombra de Ulises.*

British Library Cataloguing in Publication Information Available

Library of Congress Cataloging-in-Publication Data

Aguilar Rivera, José Antonio, 1968–
        [Sombra de Ulises. English]
        The shadow of Ulysses : public intellectual exchange across the U.S.–Mexico border /
José Antonio Aguilar Rivera ; with a foreword by Russell Jacoby.
        p.   cm.
        Includes bibliographical references and index.
        ISBN 0-7391-0173-0 (alk. paper)
        1. Mexico—Intellectual life—20th century. 2. Intellectuals—Mexico—History—20th
century. 3. United States—Intellectual life—20th century. 4. Intellectuals—United
States—History—20th century. 5. Mexico—Relations—United States. 6. United States—
Relations—Mexico. I. Title.

F1234 .A23513   2000
303.48'273072—dc21   00-041954

Printed in the United States of America

The paper used in this publication meets the minimum requirements of American
National Standard for Information Sciences—Permanence of Paper for Printed Library
Materials, ANSI/NISO Z39.48–1992.

This book is dedicated to Russell Jacoby

And what should they know of England who only England know?

Rudyard Kipling

Contents

Foreword

Mexico garners attention in the United States with stories of violence, drugs, illegal immigration, and sometimes elections. Its intellectual life only occasionally sparks notice—and when it does, attention is confined to a few writers like Octavio Paz and Carlos Fuentes. Why? In the era of globalization and multiculturalism Americans have become intellectually more provincial. Our ethnic restaurants get better but our thinking gets worse or, at least, smaller. Earlier generations of American authors with inferior restaurants seemed more cosmopolitan. In the nineteenth century, writers like Washington Irving and William Prescott wrote often about Spanish America. In the first decades of the twentieth century droves of American intellectuals visited and explored Mexico—not only radicals like Frank Tannenbaum, but writers like Hart Crane and Katherine Anne Porter, photographers like Edward Weston, as well as philosophers like John Dewey. In the twenties and thirties, according to one historian, an "enormous vogue of things Mexican," symbolized by a 1929 Madison Square Garden pageant called Aztec Gold, swept the United States.[1]

Nor was this a one-way street. Mexican artists visited the United States and its intellectuals followed the debates in New York (and Paris). As Mauricio Tenorio Trillo has noted, in the mid-twentieth century Mexico captured the imagination of many American and European intellectuals, but the attention went both ways. "The issues discussed in Mexico in those days paralleled the ones debated in New York or the radical Parisian cafes: social revolution, cultural exhaustion of the West, the problems of industrialization, rural peoples and revolution, and the rediscovery of natives and non-Westerners in arts and politics."[2] Some of the discussion centered around *Contemporáneos*, an avant-garde magazine founded in 1928 that served as a forum for Mexican and European writers. In fact, *Contemporáneos* frequently riled Mexican observers by being too cosmopolitan.[3] It is the spirit of *Contemporáneos* that animates this book by José Antonio Aguilar Rivera.

The eroding intellectual contact between Mexico and the United States has stirred Aguilar Rivera to write *The Shadow of Ulysses*, a provocative series of reflections on Mexican and American writers. Aguilar Rivera is a young political scientist who received his doctorate from the University of Chicago and presently teaches at CIDE (Centro de Investigación y Docencia Económicas) in Mexico City, where he was born. He is a rare scholar who is completely at home in both Mexican and American intellectual life. In fact, part of the problem he addresses is the scarcity of intellectuals who easily crisscross this border. The prominence of Fuentes and now Jorge Castañeda, he writes, is partly the result of their ability to address an American audience in fluid English. Aguilar Rivera has some tough-minded things to say about Castañeda (and Enrique Krauze) yet his chief desire is to invigorate a lagging discussion and to overcome the "mutual intellectual neglect" that has recently marked the relations of the United States and Mexico. He is also clear: scholarly knowledge of Mexico continues to accumulate in academic departments and think tanks, but fails to translate into public writings and discussion.

In 1960, C. Wright Mills, the leftist sociologist, visited the National Autonomous University of Mexico. Aguilar Rivera considers this visit as the last vital exchange between American and Mexican intellectuals. For cultural and political sustenance Mills was turning to Spanish America; he traveled to Cuba; wrote about the Cuban revolution in *Listen, Yankee*; and acknowleged his Mexican friends in his book *The Marxists*. Fuentes in turn dedicated *The Death of Artemio Cruz* to Mills. But soon thereafter, according to Aguilar Rivera, the Mexican-American conversation breaks down. Mills has few successors. What happened? The shift in global politics has something to do with it. Revolution lost its allure, although recent events in Chiapas suggest the romance in social upheaval is not completely dead. Yet even as their cities become more and more Latino, North American intellectuals turn toward Paris or London, not Mexico City.

Aguilar Rivera does not have all the answers, but he has many salient questions. He also steps on toes; points with fingers; calls people names. This is all to the good. We need impolite treatises to reawaken our dormant discussion. Perhaps Aguilar Rivera's book will help rekindle a conversation that has been cold for too long. More power to him.

Russell Jacoby
UCLA
April 2000

Notes

1. See generally Helen Delpar, *The Enormous Vogue of Things Mexican: Cultural Relations between the United States and Mexico, 1920-1935* (Tuscaloosa: University of Alabama Press, 1992). The phrase "the enormous vogue of things Mexican" actually derives from a 1933 *New York Times* article, commenting on the American fascination with Mexico (55). See also Henry C. Schmidt, "The American Intellectual Discovery of Mexico in the 1920s," *South Atlantic Quarterly,* 77 (1978): 335-351.

2. Mauricio Tenorio Trillo, "South of the Border: Mexico in the American Imagination, 1914-1947/Mexico en la imaginacion NorteAmericana: 1914-1947," *Latin American Research Review* 32 (summer 1997): 224.

3. See Edward John Mullen, Jr., "A Study of *Contemporáneos*: A Revista Mexicana de Cultura (1928-1931)," unpublished Ph.D. dissertation (Northwestern University, 1968).

Introduction

Ourselves with Others

"It is very difficult," Tocqueville once said, "to make the inhabitants of democracies listen if you are not talking about them."[1] The chapters that follow not only are not entirely devoted to the United States, but also do not fall neatly in any ready-made category. This is not a book about American intellectuals. Nor about Mexicans. It is about ourselves with others. As the title suggests, I undertook an exploration on a cultural frontier that has seldom been charted. This is also an effort to reconnect the experiences of two distant neighbors. In looking into the abyss that separates both countries, I've come to realize its depth and width. However, I could hardly imagine the difficulties that such a hybrid condition would pose to the publication of the book in the United States. Not only do we know little about each other, we simply do not want to know. When it comes to national certainties it is far easier to rely on prejudices. Even the very crudest of them, allow me to quote Tocqueville again, "take an unconscionable time to efface, in spite of all the froth and stir of men and things."[2]

Is there such a thing as a binational imagination? I believe so. At least, once upon a time there was. Rebuilding the fallen bridges between Mexico and the United States is an ambitious undertaking. It seems to be a task for a few cantankerous writers and scholars who are undeterred by the material hardships entailed by the endeavor. Yet I sincerely believe that Americans and Mexicans have historically suffered from mutual intellectual neglect. The consequences of such indifference are not small or negligible. Similar trends in both countries have gone unnoticed. For instance, Mexico and the United States have often been in the throws of nostalgia. "Nostalgia," writes Christopher Lasch, "not to be equated simply with the remembrance of things past, is better understood as an abdication of memory."[3] Nostalgic impulses denaturalize the past by obscuring the links between yesterday and today. Dreaming of "the way we were" prevents the imaginative reconstruction of the past. A study of the past requires an exercise in memory. In the pages that follow,

I try to steer clear of nostalgic traps and the facile idea that the past was somehow "better" or "richer." Nevertheless, it does seem to me that we have lost some of the virtues that once animated intellectual life in Mexico and the United States. This lament is not resignation. What has been lost can be retrieved.

In the Mexican intellectual tradition, jeremiads are not well looked upon because they tend "to sterilize expression and action from the public sphere."[4] Puritanical moralizing is antithetical to the exigencies of politics, or the art of the possible. The United States, on the other hand, is the land of jeremiads: a very peculiar type of lament that has occupied the national imaginary for a very long time. It bewails the failure to live up to its presumed national ideals. Melodrama aside, Mexicans could learn much from this type of self-flagellation.

Jeremiads, dating back to the Puritan era, warn of the dangers of decay, to the community, the nation, and the individual. Historically, they serve as calls to action in the face of conformity. They also reveal the great impatience of American society with the present. Americans tend to have very high personal moral yardsticks, while Mexicans can be faulted for an excessive complacency with one another.

The spirit of this lament seems appropriate in reflection upon the decay of the intellectual life in Mexico and the United States. In an earlier time—perhaps a better one—bridges connected the experiences of both communities which shared the hope that reason would serve to transform the world into a better place. The dream is over and today it appears intelligence has been taken hostage. The concerns of intellectuals are narrower than before and more petty. Public debate has ended; discussion is full of vituperation and diatribe. In the process, we have all lost.

A full account of this late-twentieth-century phenomenon would require a study of the very different roles that intellectuals play in each country and where very different "representations" of intellectuals exist.[5] Intellectuals can be defined as individuals endowed with the ability to *represent*: to embody or articulate a message, vision, attitude, philosophy, or opinion before a public. With this definition in mind, we can say that the level of discussion and public role of the intellectuals have suffered a marked decline. In both Mexico and the United States, reflection today is much more narrow. Specialization is the norm. The universalistic vocation, according to Edward Said, means "taking a risk in order to go beyond the easy certainties provided by our background, language, nationality, which so often shields us from the realities of others. It also means looking for and trying to uphold a single standard for human behavior."[6]

The definition of an "intellectual" could be broadened *ad infinitum* to include virtually everyone. Artists, journalists, librarians, and others are, in a real way, intellectuals. Such an expansive definition, however, will not do for the task at hand. Aware that some of the richness of the concept will be lost by restricting it, I see no other way around this dilemma. My focus is strictly on *public intellectuals,* regardless of their formation and/or discipline: they could be, and are, novelists, political scientists, sociologists, historians, and poets. Public intellectuals, according to Russell Jacoby, are those that direct their energies at the larger, educated, nonspecialized, reading public interested in broader themes and issues.

This book aims at exploring intellectual exchanges between the United States and Mexico from the 1920s to the present. It is an effort to compare changes in the role of intellectuals in the two countries over the same period, changes which have affected this dialogue. Real intellectual debate, I argue, which was present in both countries up until the 1960s, has all but disappeared. In the United States it declined with the growth of academe, particularly as those engaged in intellectual protest in the 1960s were absorbed into the universities, and public intellectuals became experts and professors. In Mexico, something of the same happened, following the Tlatelolco massacre of 1968. Would-be intellectuals of the left turned to Marxism and its derivatives and were absorbed into academic institutions, and though the tradition of public intellectuals in Mexico has continued, true debate over ideas has declined and turned more into personal conflicts. The U.S. experience is the mirror image of the Mexican experience: whereas U.S. intellectuals became specialized academic experts, Mexican intellectuals have become superstars of ideas who trivialize intellectual debate. This book is also an attempt to reconnect both experiences.

We are experiencing, in the words of Lasch, "a revolt of the elites."[7] Elites fulfill their role as public intellectuals less effectively today, often shunning their responsibilities altogether. The dangers of this revolt are obvious, where reason recedes, demagoguery reigns; and where reflection withers, violent emotions rule. What has taken place in both countries can only be characterized as a progressive "barbarization." Along with declining standards of living, we see the demise of the social bases that once engendered a rich community life in America. Mexico in turn, is plagued by crime and political upheaval. Democracy there is but a fragile newborn. In both countries there is a clear sense of malaise. The pages that follow touch on many sensitive issues and some will disagree with what I have to say about today's intellectual climate. This seems unavoidable. My aim is to explain, not to please.

Some caveats are in order. This book does not pretend to be an intellectual history of either Mexico or the United States. Many issues are treated only tangentially, while others are completely omitted. The reader will not find a rigorous anatomical study of "Homo Plubicus," in either country. In the course of the book, I may have committed more than a single injustice in what I have to say. This work is also not a compendium of the countless debates that have animated Mexican intellectual life over the last fifty years. Some of these debates, not mentioned here, warrant extended discussion, such as the controversial decision by the federal government to present a very different reading of "the official story" in its national textbooks. These issues, as well as a comparative approach to multiculturalism, are well documented elsewhere.

The book is written in two parts. Part 1 (chapters 1 and 2) develops the overall argument. Chapter 1 describes the bridge that once connected the intellectual experience of the two countries. Chapter 2 contrasts the earlier moment with the contemporary situation, characterized by a simultaneous intellectual crisis. I trace the collapse of the bridge and the ensuing absence of dialogue. Part 2 (chapters 3 and 4) is devoted to two Mexicans swimming against the tide and maintaining an open line of communication with both intellectual worlds: Carlos Fuentes and Jorge G. Castañeda. Both are *avis raris*. They also exemplify how we may build new and more lasting bridges. Mexican and American intellectuals need to open themselves to the world and emerge from their cocoons. We all have much to learn from one another. Observing another reality across the river could be a way for U.S. intellectuals to reclaim their place in the public arena and for Mexicans to become more rigorous and professional. In both nations, far too much cultural apathy has taken place.

While I originally wrote the book in Spanish, I kept in mind the American reader as well. However, several sections of the manuscript have been rewritten for the English version. I am profoundly indebted to Rose Hocker and Emiliano Corral, my translators. They, among all, were the first to believe in this project. My deepest gratitude goes to Rose, for her generosity and enthusiasm; she put many hours of tiresome work on a difficult text. I would also like to thank many other generous friends and colleagues who read parts of the manuscript and offered helpful criticism: Mauricio Tenorio, Charles Hale, Javier Garcíadiego, Marteen Van Doren, Jesús Silva Herzog Márquez, Rafael Rojas, and María del Carmen Gastélum. I am also indebted to several anonymous reviewers. Emiliano Corral and Sergio Sáenz provided critical help in the revision of the manuscript. Research for this book was conducted with the aid of a grant of the Mexico-U.S. Fund for Culture (sponsored by the Rockefeller Foundation, the FONCA, and the Fundación Cultural Bancomer of Mexico) that was awarded to me in 1995. The Spanish version won the Alfonso Reyes Prize in 1997.

Had I not read *The Last Intellectuals* as a graduate student at The University of Chicago, perhaps this book may not have been written. It is a great pleasure to acknowledge my debt to Russell Jacoby: a splendid historian, a benevolent friend, and an indomitable champion of intellectual honesty and uncompromising criticism. He was and still is a source of inspiration to me. This book is dedicated to him.

Perhaps the image of an intellectual bridge between Mexico and the United States is only a dream, a cultural chimera. Alexis de Tocqueville once wrote: "no men are less dreamers than the citizens of a democracy."[8] For once, I hope he was wrong.

Notes

1. Alexis de Tocqueville, *Democracy in America* (New York: Harper & Row, 1988), 642.

2. Tocqueville, *Democracy in America,* 640.

3. Christopher Lasch, *The True and Only Heaven: Progress and Its Critics* (New York: W. W. Norton, 1991), 14.

4. Carlos Fuentes, "Los escritores y la política," *Plural,* 13 (October 1972), 27.

5. Edward Said, *Representations of the Intellectual: The 1993 Reith Lecture* (New York: Pantheon Books, 1994).

6. Said, *Representations of the Intellectual,* xvi.

7. Christopher Lasch, *The Revolt of the Elites and the Betrayal of Democracy* (New York: W. W. Norton, 1995).

8. Tocqueville, *Democracy in America,* 598.

Part One

Chapter 1

A Tale of Two Countries

He rests. He has traveled.
Ulysses, James Joyce

Frank Tannenbaum, American historian, political analyst, and activist, wrote in 1924, "There is a future in Mexico, a cultural future that may well prove the greatest Renaissance in the contemporary world."[1] Tannenbaum expressed an enthusiasm for the Mexican Revolution that many other intellectuals shared.[2] The beginning of the twenties offered new horizons of what was possible. Revolutionary experiments held a certain fascination.[3] They were seen as laboratories, where history was defied and new techniques for social transformation were tested, promising to do away with ancestral injustices. As few times before in history, the hope of regeneration seemed to be sustained by recent events. In Russia, a new society was being constructed and the socialist experiment had not yet awakened the doubts that Stalin's purges would produce years later. It seemed the forces of destiny could be molded according to human will.

And the revolution of the Bolsheviks was not the only one attracting intellectuals' attention. The Mexican Revolution made "the folks next door" interesting again for Americans, particularly for radicals and reformists. Once the armed phase was over, revolutionaries began the program of national reconstruction. This endeavor found support and sympathy in the United States. For American reformist intellectuals, Mexico held a rather quaint attraction, it was a preindustrial country that was immersed in a "profound process of social change and self-discovery."[4] The enthusiasm was shared by Carleton Beals, Ernest Gruening, John Dewey, Bertram D. Wolfe, Katherine Anne Porter, and Alma Reed, among others.

3

Once upon a Bridge

American intellectuals' interest in Mexico preceded the revolution. The "interactive" moments, as Mauricio Tenorio calls the contacts between the budding social sciences in the United States and Mexico, are replete with shared influences and cultural undertakings.[5] For example Franz Boas, one of the most influential figures in American anthropology in the first half of the century, fostered the creation, in Mexico, of the International School of Anthropology and Ethnology (*Escuela Internacional de Antropología y Etnología*), which was inaugurated in 1910, during celebrations of the Mexican Independence Centennial.[6] One of Boas' disciples was the Mexican anthropologist Manuel Gamio (1883-1960). In 1922 at Columbia University, Gamio became the first Mexican to earn a doctorate.[7] Boas' culturalist theories were pragmatically employed by Gamio in the construction of postrevolutionary indigenism, which for years would be the official doctrine of the new regime.[8] While Boas wanted science to serve in the demythification of racial tradition, Gamio sought to put it to work for a "particular version of Mexican nationalism," which would allow for the *integration* of Indians into the Mexican nation-state.[9] Thus, specialized knowledge became a useful tool in Gamio's political career. According to Mauricio Tenorio, Boas and his Mexican disciple complemented each other: "Boas wanted science to be the tool for universal demystification of old racial myths and his own source of authority and fame. Gamio desired the latter end for himself as well, but as an instrument of a version of Mexican nationalism—the incorporation of Indians into modern national development and the incorporation of Mexico into the concert of modern nations." Both saw mutual advantage in their intellectual exchage:

> Boas needed Gamio's anthropology to support the study of tradition and primitivism and to achieve a truly professional science, universal and cosmopolitan. . . . Gamio needed Boasian anthropology, theoretically, to advance his belief in the feasibility of modernity for a mestizo nation, and, politically, to consolidate his own influence through his links with international science.[10]

The relationship between Boas and Gamio can be seen as one of the hanging bridges that united the two countries, albeit precariously, in the twenties and thirties. Certainly, the link was fragile because it was built from personal relationships. Nonetheless, over those rudimentary bridges crossed a great number of ideas. In both countries, these ideas found expression in programs and policies that would significantly transform the two societies. A series of binational fascinations seemed to center on the figure of John Dewey. As Tenorio states, the philosophical, epistemological, political, and institutional roots of contemporary American social sciences can be traced back to the philosopher and educator's influence.[11] It is impossible to do justice to all the ideas of the American philosopher here, but suffice it to mention a few. Dewey thought that absolute truths did not exist in religion, philosophy, or politics. He was committed to a morality where what mattered were the real-world consequences of one's actions. As the one who would systematize pragmatism, Dewey distrusted metaphysics and wanted to find the basis for moral decisions in the scientific method. Education had a tangible political end: it was to serve in the formation of a democracy.[12] Dewey's eyes were upon the future; therefore, the "old" did not excite him much. This belief in the ability of reason to solve social problems was in harmony with the spirit of the era.

The obsession with progress found fertile field in Mexico, for there, everything seemed to be reinventing itself after the violent fall of the old regime. Hence, Dewey carefully observed the postrevolutionary development of Mexico. For obvious reasons, the educational reforms undertaken by the new government sparked his interest. Furthermore, a Mexican named Moisés Sáenz (1888-1941) had been a disciple of Dewey's at the Teachers College of Columbia University. Sáenz came from a Protestant family from northern Mexico. He studied education in Jalapa, and after receiving his doctorate at Columbia, he pursued his studies at the Sorbonne in Paris. In the revolutionary public administration, Sáenz filled the positions of Guanajuato state director of education, director of the National Preparatory School (*Escuela Nacional Preparatoria*), and in 1924, he was named assistant secretary of Public Education (*subsecretario de Educación Pública*) for six years.[13] Sáenz was the creator of the ambitious rural education program that the triumphant revolutionaries undertook in the twenties. The earnestness of their intentions was reflected in the budget. In 1923, the government allocated to education 15 percent of its total budget, a figure that has rarely been surpassed in following years of postrevolutionary stability.[14] Regeneration in the most backward social sectors of the country required an extraordinary effort in education. The task consisted of taking the instruments of progress to the most remote and far-off regions in Mexico. The construction workers in this engineering project would be rural teachers. For Sáenz, Dewey's ideas offered a program of concrete action. These ideas could not have come at a better time for Mexico, since the country was trying to put its human infrastructure back together. Thus, revolution and pragmatism met in the plan for rural education. The task of national reconstruction in Mexico led to a singular opening to the world outside. According to Enrique Krauze, being Protestant in a predominantly Catholic country must have made Sáenz "in some ways a marginal Mexican."[15] Sáenz was Dewey's most illustrious and direct interpreter, but he certainly was not the only one. The interest was not an isolated episode: it went further than simply a personal relationship between teacher and student. Mexican educators participated in a worldwide revisionist movement; with the task of their revolution behind them, they found themselves in the avant-garde of educational experimentation.[16]

One tool of the new pedagogy inspired by Dewey was the school "of action"; a place where children learned to work and live, and "only secondarily to read and write."[17] Dewey thought that new problems could not be adequately resolved through the application of ideas and principles that had been created to solve other, different problems. Mexican children's difficulties were of a practical nature: they needed to learn how to cultivate and carry on their social relationships with other members of the community. The school would be the People's House (*Casa del Pueblo*), the perfect place for socialization. As Sáenz explained to a group of Texan teachers, "We have an urgent need to integrate our country, to create this community of interests, ideals and sentiments called patriotism."[18]

According to Krauze, the one who had the idea of importing Dewey's "school of action" to Mexico was not Sáenz, but rather José Vasconcelos,[19] "who, to those ends, sent a young Mexican teacher, Eulalia Guzmán, to study the 'learn by doing' method in the United States."[20] Upon her return to Mexico, Guzmán wrote an informative booklet, *La escuela nueva o de la acción* (The New or Action School), which served to spread Dewey's pedagogical principles in Mexico.[21] Although, in Mexico, the animosity Vasconcelos felt for Dewey's ideas is well known, this antagonism did not develop until some time later.[22] During the first years Vasconcelos spent at the head of the Public Education Ministry (*Secretaría de Educación Pública*), he criticized teachers' traditional methods. In 1922, he wrote that primary schools:

> [Have become too often] a sort of elemental university, in which the teacher must pretend to be the most daring of walking encyclopedias, with the consequence that the child receives all knowledge reduced and deformed, since only the rarest of geniuses could teach well, at once, singing, drawing, gym, mathematics, natural history, etc. . . . The unity which the old system presupposes, the old system in which the normalist professor with his bookish methodologies imparts all types of teachings, was the unity of a trivial encyclopedism, imposing his points of view on the malleable childish imaginations; it was the unity of pedantry, of narrowness, and conventionality, of which so frequently suffocates schools.[23]

Dewey's imprint can be seen in these lines. In the same way, Vasconcelos promoted an educational reform that sought to make teaching more hands-on. In general, teachers responded favorably to the implantation on a national level of active schooling, after an initial period of uneasiness, due to the relative newness of the project and a lack of information. "To fill this lack, in 1923, '*Bases para la Organización de la Escuela Conforme al Principio de la Acción*' (Fundamentals for the Organization of School in Accordance with the Principle of Action), was published."[24] Through Sáenz, Dewey's ideas had a decisive influence on the rural schools project of the new regime.

During the Vasconcelos period, a new social pedagogy took shape. The distinctive characteristic of this current of thought would be the Deweyian idea of progress. Soon this philosophy entered into conflict with the Christian spirituality of the members of the Ateneo de la Juventud circle.[25] However, even he could not help but be pleased with some aspects of the new education system.[26] Before 1920, Caso had criticized the way basic education was imparted. "In Mexican schools, no work is done." Among the solutions he proposed was "encouraging children to *act* constantly, to use up their physical energy."[27] In practical matters, Vasconcelos agreed with Sáenz on many points, for example, on the functional and practical character of learning, and on the supreme importance of morality. But while for Vasconcelos this was necessary it was by no means sufficient. An educational system could not be conceived of in solely practical terms; it had to have a deeper function, in which esthetic emotion and spiritual intuition would have to play an important role.[28]

Dewey, who was interested in the political, social, and intellectual development in Mexico, visited the country on two occasions. In 1926, he was invited by Sáenz, who was then assistant secretary of Education (*subsecretario de Educación*) under the government of President Calles. During the summer of that year, Dewey lectured at the National University (*Universidad Nacional Autónoma de México*).[29] The second visit came about in April 1937, when the American philosopher was at the head of the famous commission, which, in Coyoacán, Mexico City, judged and exonerated Leon Trotsky of the charges Stalin had laid against him.[30]

Dewey wrote about several aspects of Mexican society. He concentrated on the relationship between church and state, about the educational reforms of the twenties, and about the democratic prospects of postrevolutionary Mexico.[31] Aside from the published accounts, Tenorio has found Dewey's ideas and commentaries regarding his trips to Mexico in letters and other commentaries. Dewey saw Mexico as a laboratory where his ideas were being put to the test. Sáenz, for his part, held his personal laboratory to be the indigenous villages where teachers' universal ideas could be used as an innovating instrument for achieving the integration of the indigenous communities into the nation as a whole. Dewey looked upon these experiments in Mexico with interest and pleasure, but maintained an ambivalent opinion over the authoritarian Mexican regime:

> As if democracy, as he believed, was not a universal conclusion and a normative parameter. Mexico and its social and educational experiments were in fact a difficult test for Dewey's ideas: his scientific and philosophical ideas were being, he believed, applied, showing their universalism and utility; but democracy, the most normative and universal part of his thought, was not included in the experiment, and Dewey knew it but showed not much concern, as if the formula science-democracy was only reproducible in its natural scenario, the U.S.[32]

However, soon after, this formula would be attacked in the very place where it originated, where science would be seen by some as an inadequate and insufficient foundation for democracy.

Return to Babel

In 1930, Robert Maynard Hutchins, then president of the University of Chicago, imported Mortimer Adler from Columbia University. Adler had become famous for his work on the Great Books, a compendium of the most important works of Western civilization. For fifteen years, Hutchins, Adler, and others in Chicago were devoted to teaching and publishing the Great Books. In 1940, along with *Encyclopedia Britannica*, the University of Chicago published the Great Books in a single collection, a series that covered from Homer to Freud. Three decades later, the collection, in its original English, would be distributed throughout Mexico with some success.

In the thirties, the clouds of totalitarian ideologies were gathering on the horizon. Within democratic states there were no certainties. If democracy was based solely on the consent of individuals, what made this system morally superior to fascism and communism? As the enthroning of Hitler would demonstrate shortly thereafter, a totalitarian option could be freely consented to by the people. The specter of the fall of the Republic of Weimar was thus converted into the obsession of a generation of intellectuals who, like Leo Strauss and Hannah Arendt, emigrated to the United States before the war. The scientific method, however powerful it may have been, could not serve as the moral foundation for the preservation of democratic regimes.

From his post at the University of Chicago, Hutchins contended that the inner reinforcement of democracies entailed a conscious return to absolute principles. And these principles had not varied since the time of Plato and Aristotle.[33] Democracy was firmly anchored in a transcendental foundation. This return to fundamental values implied the rejection of pragmatism, relativism, and utilitarianism. Dewey had become the very symbol of these and other theories that rejected the idea of natural law. All of a sudden, the philosopher and his followers were no longer the intellectual vanguard, and they found themselves, to their surprise, increasingly on the defensive. Dewey rejected Hutchins' proposal of a return to the Greeks and the Middle Ages as misguided. For Dewey, this was a reactionary attempt to seek guidelines from societies in which there was very little social democracy and very precarious knowledge of scientific principles.[34] The progressive option, according to Dewey, was to look forward and accept science as the transformative force that could turn modern democratic ideals into reality. It was precisely in education that science could contribute to the realization of these ideals. Dewey became, subsequently, the father of what would be called "new" education. Socially, progressive education was part of a wider effort "to liberate individuals and institutions from the shackles of oppressive ways of life." This effort had an inherent contention with the past. As Dewey himself said,

> It should be a commonplace, but unfortunately it is not, that no education, or any-thing else for that matter, is progressive unless it is making progress. Nothing is more reactionary in its consequences than the effort to live according to the ideas, principles, customs, habits or institutions which at some time in the past represented a change for the better but which in the present constitute factors in the problems confronting us.[35]

In Mexico, after an initial period, these ideas became the anathema of the spiritual heirs of Vasconcelos. Robert Maynard Hutchins, on the other hand, would have struck Vasconcelos as quite a fine fellow.[36] The two men nearly crossed paths at Hyde Park in the late twenties. In 1927, two years before Hutchins would become president of the University of Chicago, Vasconcelos was invited by that institution as a visiting professor. Max Mason was presid-ing over the university at the time. Vasconcelos, former minister of Education, left Mexico in 1925 seeking exile, after being frustrated in his campaign for governor of the state of Oaxaca.[37] The pilgrimage of the prophet would in-clude various stops, among them the Holy Land and the United States. Vasconcelos' visit to Chicago was not an accident. Its university was one of the main intellectual centers of the country. The legacy of Dewey (who was in the philosophy department from 1894 to 1904) could still be felt in 1927. The Social Sciences Building, which was only half-built when Vasconcelos saw it, epitomized the American faith in the transforming power of science. That year, Dewey, then at Columbia University, published *The Public and Its Problems*, a book which articulated a widespread malaise within American society.[38] Several matters, both internal and external, were causing consterna-tion in universities. The rise of authoritarian movements in Europe worried professors to no end: the topics of international relations and diplomacy were discussed unceasingly. The crisis of parliamentary regimes inspired American universities to reflect upon the nature of liberal democracy. At the same time, there were other problems closer to home. American society was experiencing a rapid transformation; the growing fragmentation of the social body was palpable, and some doubted the capacity of the political system to incorporate the new actors. Although there was consensus over the normative value of democracy, the facts seemed to refute this on a daily basis. Reality could not be denied. On the contrary, it had to be *studied*. Science presented itself, in this context, as a resource that would serve not only to bring the wounds of the democratic ideal to light, but also to speed the transformation from theory to practice. In 1926, these ideas were articulated by the philosopher T.V. Smith in *The Democratic Way of Life*.[39] This was the prevailing intellectual environment in the United States upon Vasconcelos' arrival. The American scene was not all openness. Vasconcelos also faced prejudice. As Cockcroft asserts, several racist best-sellers were popular at the time. In 1920 T. Lothrop Stoddard asserted that Mexicans "were culturally inferior and were undesirable immigrants because they were 'born communist.'. . . A 1930 book titled *The Alien in Our Midst* offered articles championing white supremacy and claiming to demonstrate 'scientifically' that Mexicans are racially inferior."[40]

The work of the former Mexican minister of Education was probably looked upon with approving eyes by many in Chicago. He arrived at the university at the end of a cultural and spiritual odyssey. After all, the magnitude of the Mexican civilizing efforts had few precedents in the Western world. Vasconcelos was a disenchanted Prometheus who had taken on a task of social redemption worthy of Hercules. By that time, Vasconcelos had already written *La Raza Cósmica* (The Cosmic Race) in 1925, and *Indología: una Interpretación de la Cultura Iberoamericana* (Indology: an Interpretation of Iberoamerican Culture) in 1926. Christopher Domínguez is right to assert that few times before has Mexico been "a land open to the imagination of a truly New World,"[41] as it was in the years when Vasconcelos reigned and laid out plans.

In the summer of 1926, precisely when Dewey was in Mexico, José Vasconcelos and Manuel Gamio, both former civil servants, each gave speeches at the Harris Foundation discussing the "problems of Mexico." Both were included in the book, *Aspects of Mexican Civilization*, published by the University of Chicago in December of that same year. A second book, *Some Mexican Problems*, would include a text of the still assistant secretary of Education (*subsecretario de Educación*) Moisés Sáenz.[42] Vasconcelos titled his speech, "The Latin American Basis of Mexican Civilization," very representative of the spirit inspiring him during that period.[43]

The United States' preoccupation with international relations ensured that the texts by Gamio and Vasconcelos were received with interest. Vasconcelos explicitly recognized "the hospitality of this University of Chicago, a hospitality generously granted to truth and the good cause of human understanding." In the first part of his speech entitled, "Similarity and Contrast," Vasconcelos described Mexico as a land where the cycles of creation and destruction impeded the progressive advance of civilization: "Even the wise of every period find themselves unable to take advantages of the cultural conquests of the preceding epoch."[44] This is why Mexico, just as a large part of Latin America, was simultaneously a country of hope and despair. Between the Anglo-Saxons in the north and the Latins in the south there is a "deep, important difference." This difference was the spiritual character, found "in the manner of feeling and in the manner of expressing our feelings of life. It is in the type of our higher desires and in the manner we go about our pleasures that we can best be distinguished on from the other." This sensualist note, it is true, evoked the image of Ariel in the land of Caliban. However, at this point Vasconcelos was still far from embracing cultural Manichaeanism. At that time cooperation and participation in a common civilizing movement were possible. Vasconcelos would say:

> We are a sort of re-adaptation of the Mediterranean standards and manners of life while the North Americans are a sort of enlarged Baltic civilization. And the fact that European civilization is a solidly inspired forward movement of humanity, notwithstanding the internal differences of Europe, indeed exactly on account of those internal differences, should teach us in America that it is possible to build a strong powerful civilization of the New World without trying to impose one type of civilization upon the other, without trying even to argue which is the better, whether the Latin or the Anglo-Saxon; for both are useful, and perhaps both are indispensable for the present and the future power and glory of the continent.[45]

It would be very easy to cast these ideas aside as the words of a polite and mannerly visitor. Nevertheless, none of this is inconsistent with the faith Vasconcelos had in the cosmic race. Rather, in these ideas we can perceive an explicit acknowledgment of shared human experience. "It is not by suppressing differences," Vasconcelos said, "that progress opens its way; it is through differences, deeply inspired, sincere differences, that the human soul has made all of its conquests."[46] Only material differences create bitterness and rivalry among men. Spiritual ones, on the contrary, tend to strengthen human bonds, "because we find pleasure in every difference of the taste; and every peculiarity enriches the wealth of the species." Here Vasconcelos, with singular mastery, translated an idealist argument into the practical language of Americans. The notion of "cultural capital" was intelligible and attractive to an audience accustomed to accumulation:

> In itself spiritual wealth is such that everybody can enjoy it without using it up, but on the contrary the more you make use of it the richer in value it becomes. The fact that this continent is divided among Anglo-Saxons and Latins should be looked upon then as a blessing; because we all long for a higher, richer spiritual world, and it is only through the work of singularly gifted groups of people that a true all-comprehending type of civilization may come to life. The bigoted patriot who may dream of an all-Yankee America extending its shops from Patagonia to Canada is just as potent a foe to the true ends of mankind as the blind Latin-American chauvinist who may dream of a time of decay in which the Yankee standards of life are to be substituted by the newer southern manners of life.[47]

Is this a sincere Vasconcelos? Perhaps the intention to create a "new cycle in history" in the hemisphere was a little too much. But even if this cycle of "freedom, understanding, and love between all the races and nations" were just a convenient slogan, it is hard to accept the idea that Vasconcelos did not believe in the essence of what he was saying: the suggestion that the savage Caliban and the apollonian Ariel could live in harmony, and even learn a thing or two from each other. In any case, the confidence Vasconcelos, the prophet, had in the future was unshakable. "Mexico," he said, reprimanding Americans, "is not a hopeless, backward country, but a wonderful promise, more than that, a certainty that can not be delayed very much longer."[48] The date for the fulfillment of that promise was, of course, 1929.[49]

For Vasconcelos, as a future candidate for the presidency of the Republic of Mexico, it was important to refute the idea, accepted by many Americans, that only a military chieftain, or *caudillo,* could be successful in the backward Latin American countries. In the section, "Democracy in Latin America," Vasconcelos asserted: "a despotism can never survive in a clash with a democracy." Furthermore, it was the democratic form of government that had created the most long-lived and extensive empires. "There is not," he preached, "a single permanently successful case under the personal system of government." Dictatorship led to Latin American *caudillismo* or Russian Bolshevism. It was a matter of culture shock between civilizations, between "orientalism" and the "European and Christian way of life." These words had a dual purpose; on the one hand they were meant to comfort the citizens of an uncertain democracy, and on the other they were intended to translate democratic faith to the southern part of the continent. The theory that democracy was good for "this country but not for this or that other," said the Prophet, "has no basis in the facts." The task was still more complicated: Vasconcelos not only had to show civilians to be superior to the military, and thus dissuade the Americans from supporting another Díaz, but also he had to establish the superiority of one particular *type* of civilian, the philosopher-king. "In Mexico we have always had a fine type of man: the learned man, fully prepared with all the advantages of a college career, and all the insight of patriotism and even of genius." Later, referring to Juárez, Vasconcelos would add, "The only case in which an intellectual group actually came into power in Mexico, in all the history of Mexico, is, at the same time, the only decent period of the history of Mexico and the only progressive period."[50] This possibly explains his critical, and yet quite praising, portrait of Woodrow Wilson. However, Vasconcelos argument must have appeared rather unconvincing to Americans, who suffered from a secular distrust toward intellectuals.

In the third and final section of the former minister's lecture, he referred to the "racial problem of Latin America." The subject was not confined to Latin America. And there, Vasconcelos hit, as Alexis de Tocqueville had done nearly one hundred years before, a sensitive nerve. The idea of the integrating, while at the same time respecting, difference had clear implications for the United States. Americans were, according to Vasconcelos, a white civilization, "that may contain, and does contain, millions of [men from] other racial stocks such as the Negro, but does not consider such dissimilar stock as part of itself." In southern countries, on the other hand, "we have . . .a civilization that from the beginning accepts a mixed standard of social arrangement not only as a matter of fact but through law."[51] Here he could not resist setting forth his sermon on cosmic race: "The mestizo is always turned toward the future, he is a bridge to the future." The attempt to purify the race, to do away with the aborigine stocks, was nothing but a "case of cowardice." With a mix of approval and fear, Americans must have received the Prophet's admonition: "The so-called pure-race theory is nothing but the theory of the dominating people of every period of history." Hybridism, "in man, as well as in plants, tends to produce better types and tends to rejuvenate those types that have become static." The mestizo, or person of mixed Indian and European heritage, was clearly superior: "We are perhaps more truly universal in sentiment than any other people." However, a feeling of historic mission was lacking: "Many of our failings arise from the fact that we do not know exactly what we want." Vasconcelos said:

> No nation has ever risen to true greatness without an ardent faith in some high ideal. Democracy and equal opportunities for every man has been the motto of the great American nation. Broadness, universality of sentiment and thought, in order to fulfil the mission of bringing together all the races of the earth and with the purpose of creating a new type of civilization, is, I believe, the ideal that would give us in Latin-America strength and vision.[52]

This was Prometheus at his best. "The goal may seem too ambitious, but it is only great, unlimited ideals that are capable of giving a nation the strength that is required to break the routine of life and to outdo itself." Furthermore, the problems of *mestizaje* (miscegenation) would end up spreading. The era of pure blood was about to end. "The world," Vasconcelos said, "is coming back to the confusion of Babel."

As mentioned previously, the creed of the cosmic race found science to be an obstacle. How could one evangelize *mestizaje* against semiscientific theories on the survival of the fittest? In his antipositivist diatribe Vasconcelos claimed, "The sort of science we have been teaching in our schools was not fit for this purpose; on the contrary it was the science created to justify the aims of the conqueror and the imperialist." Those who heard Vasconcelos hurl this accusation probably lifted their brow in skepticism. Chicago, after all, was one of the temples of science: Dewey had caused science to be associated with democracy and progressive causes, apparently never again to be disassociated. For Dewey, the crisis in democracy required "the substitution of the type of intelligence that is accepted now for the intelligence embodied by the scientific method."[53] This faith would not be placed in doubt until Hutchins and the European émigrés arrived in Chicago in the early thirties. Possibly many in the audience disbelieved Vasconcelos when he stressed that, "modern scientific theories are in many cases like the religious creeds of the old days, simply the intellectual justification of fatalities of conquest and of commercial greed."[54] For the social science establishment in Chicago, surely all of this sounded very odd. Even more odd would be Vasconcelos' admonition that, "so long as pleasure and joy do not become the rule of life, we must admit that we are lost in a mistaken path. Duty is a means, knowledge is a means, effort is a means; joy and pleasure are the only ends." But the moral of this Epicurean reflection would strike them as less charming, "and there can be no joy in a civilization in which the races are separated by hatred, prejudice and misunderstanding." The new Babel must not repeat the errors of the old one; the methods that transformed that tower into a curse should be avoided. The curse of Babel began when people were incapable of understanding one another. Instead of agreeing on a common purpose, they entered into such competition and jealousy that they ended up destroying each other.[55] In the new Babel, there was no other option but to abandon the theory of racial superiority. A cooperative interracial agreement would have to be established to create a common home.

On May 15, 1927, at the Chicago council on Foreign Relations, Vasconcelos gave a second lecture on the American foreign policy toward Mexico. His speech would be collected in a volume that presented "dispassionate" opinions on the same problem.[56] In, "A Mexican's Point of View," Vasconcelos gave a historical account of the vicissitudes of Mexican policy, from the fall of Díaz until 1927. At the same time, he admitted that the Revolution had shown Mexicans that the United States as a nation was not only an imperialist power that completely ignored the moral interests of its neighbors, but also a humane community capable of feeling fondness and good will toward its southern neighbors.

The characterization Vasconcelos presented of the United States (in which the society was good but the government and special interests were bad) had a clear strategic objective. He said,

> It was easy for us to understand the two currents of opinion: one in favor of, the other against, our country. The great mass of public opinion in the United States was in favor of the Mexican revolution because it felt that Mexico was entitled to freedom and progress just as much as any nation. Only the small group whom we may call the imperialists were of the outspoken opinion that Mexico did not deserve democracy and that a brutal dictator, an iron hand, was necessary to keep down a country of half-breeds and renegades.[57]

Vasconcelos' ability to understand and manipulate the political language of the Americans is admirable. The dichotomy between the good/society, and bad/ megacapitalists touched a populist vein that was near the surface. This same tool would be used many years later by Carlos Fuentes to make himself heard and to influence public debate in the United States. Vasconcelos could, like Fuentes, and unlike the majority of Mexican intellectuals of yesterday and today, speak and write in English. He himself wrote and delivered his speeches. He was able to make the epic of the cosmic race intelligible for another society. In Chicago he not only spoke about Mexico, but also reflected upon the present and future of the United States. This was possible because Vasconcelos was a believer in the power of ideas beyond cultural differences. However, the year 1929 would inflict profound changes both in the United States and Vasconcelos. In America the Great Depression damped enthusiasm for social progress and Vasconcelos lost the presidential race, which forever embittered him.

Memory of a War on Two Fronts

In 1921, eight years before Robert Hutchins arrived in Chicago, Vasconcelos, then president of the Universidad Nacional, was already involved in gathering a collection of the "fundamental" books. Vasconcelos in the 1920s also supported "classicism," especially by teaching the Greek classics to Mexican children, and acted accordingly as Minister of Education.[58] The editions in Spanish of the "most important books in the world" were rare and incomplete. In consequence, Vasconcelos threw himself into the adventure of mass publication of the classics. "Publishing classic editions in Spanish," said the new president, would fill "a double need of patriotism and of culture: of culture because they hold that which is fundamental in man, above differences in time and race." His goal was explicit: "I would like to have the highest works brought to the humblest hands, and thereby achieve the spiritual regeneration that must precede all regeneration."[59] Thus, *The Iliad* and *The Odyssey*, were mass published, as were the works of Plato, Aeschylus, Euripides, Plotinus, Plutarch, Dante, Goethe, and Rolland, among others. For example, 38,940 copies of *The Iliad* were printed, a number far above even the copies of that work currently published in Mexico.[60] "Hispanic American countries," according to Vasconcelos, "had entered a period of vigorous and autonomous renovation," which would continue on to coalesce until the expression of Hispanic American thought reached "universality."[61] The fact that an interest in publishing and distributing the classics occurred in both countries, more or less at the same time, is surprising. It reveals something about the spiritual condition of that era. The return to the "fundamental" authors was, perhaps, a kind of anchor, thrown

down in midflight by some distraught passengers on the train of progress, as
it seemingly left everything behind in a dizzying fashion. However, for
Vasconcelos, the distribution of the classics in Mexico would not be an antidote against the liberal relativism that was leaving democracy vulnerable to the
blows of totalitarianism, the way it would be for Hutchins some years later in
the United States. Instead, to the contrary, it would be an effort toward civilization in a backward and still half-barbaric country.

In an undated article entitled "A Hundred Books," Vasconcelos acknowledged the usefulness of the Great Books approach.[62] "The nineteenth century,"
Vasconcelos asserted, "with its emphasis on practical science, made war on the
literati." "Later," he continued, "it became evident that a society without literati was simply barbaric." The new barbarians were even more dangerous than
the old ones, because they had at their disposal the means of destruction and
the power of modern technology. Illiberal education had deprived students of
what once was the core of the curriculum: good literature and philosophy.
These barbarians commanded an unheard of amount of power. They were,
simply put, a "threat to the spirit." "To rectify the deformations of the soul
brought about by technology," Vasconcelos contended, "dr. Hutchinson (*sic*),
from the University of Chicago, fancied in the United States what he called a
return to the classics. That is, the obligation of all college graduates to include
in their curricula those subjects essential to culture: World History, Philosophy,
Logic." Hence, engineers, technicians, and specialists would no longer be
"culturally blind." Vasconcelos made a veiled attack on Dewey when he asserted: "against the Hutchin's Plan stood, and still stands, the elective American system. This is an unfortunate invention of an educator who, due to his
importance and merited fame, was able to impose his misguided system. By
virtue of this method students are free to choose and order their courses." The
best American educators had revolted against "this harmful and anarchic system." "The Latin idea of starting the educating process by teaching the gen-
eralities of culture, or of at least not doing away with them," he continued,
"has gained favor among these restorers of common sense." The reading of the
Great Books was, according to Vasconcelos, "a simple and economical" way of
inculcating in students the essentials of the civilization to which "we belong."[63]

In any case, the conflict between pragmatism and humanism, which was
taking place in both nations, demonstrated the intellectual vigor of the times.
The battle was being fought in schoolrooms, not just in universities. The territories in dispute were tradition's value, the attitude toward the past, and the
role of books. The battle was being fought on two fronts. In Mexico, pragmatism and its educational proposal would end up losing in the very place they
had been attempted—in the countryside. The chronicle of the failure can be
read in Sáenz's own words. The school of action found insurmountable obstacles in the towns it was supposed to regenerate. In practice, the new schools

rarely managed to take root because the new pedagogy faced extremely adverse social conditions. The failure of the educational experiment in Carapan, Michoacán, which Sáenz documented, was repeated throughout the length and breadth of the nation.[64] Its luck was no better in the cities. Positions in the higher levels of education, such as at the National Preparatory School (*Escuela Nacional Preparatoria*) were filled by men who, like Caso and Vasconcelos, thought, contrary to Dewey, that education was the art of philosophers. The Mexican intellectual elite thus maintained itself untouched by Dewey's forming influence.

In the United States, on the other hand, the new ideas about education were not met with the same resistance. As a transforming wave, they radically changed the face of American schools. American education was remade according to Dewey's theories and civic goals. These changes were not impeded, like they were in Mexico, by sharp social and cultural differences, nor by regional fragmentation, nor by the persistence in time and space of microcosms that secularly resisted innovation and change. The paradox was that in Mexico, where a revolution had taken place, informal barriers to change were much greater than in the United States, a stable society, where large-scale social experimentation was indeed possible. This does not imply that the United States was a homogenous country or without internal differences, but instead that a certain type of social engineering had a greater chance for success there than in Mexico. The idea of progress was resisted by some, but in general it enjoyed great power in the United States.[65]

The results of the educational policies in Mexico and the United States could hardly have been otherwise. In 1921, Mexico had 14,334,780 inhabitants, of which 5,181,000 were between 5 and 19 years old; in other words, 36 percent of the total population, but the country had only 11,000 primary schools. In that year, 1,103,051 young people between 5 and 19 years of age were enrolled in primary and secondary school in Mexico; that is, 21 percent of all school-age children.[66] The comparison with what was happening during those same years in the United States is enlightening. The figures reveal the magnitude of the educational revolution taking place in that country. In 1923, the population was 111,947,000 people. Of that total, 33,363,000 individuals were between 5 and 19 years old, or 29.8 percent. Sixty-five percent of white children between the ages of 5 and 19, as well as 55 percent of black children of the same age, were enrolled in school.[67] This means that two-thirds of American school-age youth went to school, compared to only one-fifth in Mexico. In spite of the uneven impact in Mexico in the twenties, the ideas of "new education" unquestionably received, at first, greater acceptance among teachers than did the positions of Vasconcelos and Caso, which seemed to teachers, "too far from immediate reality and pressing social problems."[68]

The overriding need to place education at the service of progress was one of the priorities of educators in both countries. Therefore, traditional teaching methods had to be revised. In the past, Dewey said, "reading had been the only road to knowledge, the only instrument capable of ensuring control over the spiritual resources that civilization had accumulated."[69] The scientific method had simply not been available to most people. Since observation and experimentation were inaccessible, it had not been possible to expose children directly to the materials of life and nature. This contact had had to be mediated through books, where great minds had interpreted and assimilated those "materials." This "regime" of intellectual authority in political, moral, and cultural matters had been necessary then because methods of scientific investigation and verification had not been developed or were in the hands of only a few.[70] "We often fail to see that the dominant position occupied by book-learning in school education is simply a corollary and relic of this epoch of intellectual development." This statement held devastating implications for the tradition that honored books as nearly sacred objects: it was a kind of secular desecration. For Dewey, "the capital handed down from past generations, and upon whose transmission the integrity of civilization depends, is no longer amassed in these banks termed books, but is in active and general circulation, at an extremely low rate of interest." The monetary metaphor he used was not gratuitous: "capital," "bank," and "interest rates" belied a simultaneous process of democratization of knowledge, and of its conversion into a purchasable object. Intellectual pragmatism claimed that books were a bitter, aristocratic aftertaste from a bygone time of prescientific darkness. Due to the obsolescence of books as vehicles of inherited knowledge, their usefulness in general education should be reconsidered. Active education, which did not place excessive emphasis on books, would be the new method of transmitting knowledge.

The concept of pragmatism made its way down to Mexico and established itself in rural schools. Speaking about new rural education, Sáenz would explain to Texan teachers:

> Reading, writing and arithmetic can only be instruments for achieving more fundamental things in life. Besides these lessons, there are other activities that are just as important, if not more so. Children in these schools have to take care of hens and chickens, cultivate their little orchards, plant their flowers, and, in addition, girls have sewing, embroidering and knitting lessons.[71]

These new schools set out to give "active and functional education," and were the epitome "of the assertion learning by doing." What was happening to Mexico, according to Sáenz, was that it was suffering the "angst of unattained ideals." Making, building, the new nation tangibly and concretely was to forge a fatherland. Here, the transcendental dimension of the process of constructing the nation was secondary. "Our problem in Mexico," Sáenz stated openly, "is not, after all, a problem of philosophy. I believe we have a satisfactory philosophy, and if we did not, it would not be difficult to import one. After all, ideas are cheap." What there was too much of were ideas, and what there was too little of were the means to act on them: "in these days of cheap and massive production of books, the best ideas in the world can be obtained in any library, and if one happens to be missing, it can be sent for, for 50 cents."[72] For Sáenz, there was no Platonic cave from which to emerge. Ideas were not the product of a laborious life devoted to knowledge and wisdom. And they were not the exclusive property of a few privileged beings. Ideas were floating around freely, just as Dewey said, in the marketplace. Upon lowering ideas to mere consumer goods, cheap ones at that, the philosophical component of education, which from the time of the Greeks had been essential in the task of teaching and learning, was devalued. There was here, also, a peculiar form of belief in the power of human's will, thanks to which the intellectual resources of humanity were up for the taking.

A battle for the soul of the culture was being waged in Mexico. This new education was, and the philosophical premises on which it rested were, attacked vehemently by Vasconcelos. As has been mentioned previously, the conflict did not begin immediately, as, for a period, Dewey's ideas were regarded with a mixture of bewilderment and hope. It was not the techniques of "learning by doing" that provoked the intellectual reaction against Dewey (after all, it did no harm for children in the remotest parts of the country to learn at school how to take to care of hens), but rather the vision of man and of civilization that was *behind* active education that was offensive.

Furthermore, resentment is retrospective. It was not until Vasconcelos wrote *De Robinson a Odiseo* (From Robinson to Odiseus) in 1935, eight years after his stay in Chicago, that the allegation against Dewey would take concrete form. The characters in this diatribe lived in two time periods at once. "I have symbolized in Robinson the astute, improvising and exclusively technical method that characterized the Anglo-Saxon era of the world." Conceived as a cultural antidote, and as if purging a momentary pragmatic weakness, Vasconcelos admonished, "now that the drunkenness of bad wine has passed, we shall return to the good wine of our tradition, and resuscitate Odiseus to set him up against the plainess of the Robinsons."[73] This dichotomy of the Anglo-Saxon/barbarian and the Latin/civilized was not, as we have seen, original. At the turn of the century, José Enrique Rodó (1871-1917), from Uruguay, had already warned against the materialist depredation of the savage Caliban in his work, *Ariel*.[74]

At the same time as Hutchins, still in Chicago, was insisting upon the need to read and sell the classics, Vasconcelos, in Mexico, maintained: "We need a classic totalism in this hour of reconstructions and universality. Robinsonism, positivism, philosophy of the road, we must complement this with the theory of the ends, the metaphysics of blessed disinterest and the conquest of the absolute."[75] The idea of the "virginal" purity of children, Vasconcelos asserted, had not been invented by Dewey (it was a notion of Rousseau's, "man was born free, but everywhere finds himself in chains"), but it had indeed been "dogmatized" by the American philosopher.

This was a frontal attack, in a battle where no prisoners would be taken. According to Vasconcelos, the warriors must be the very teachers playing the sacred role of "priests of knowledge." Culture was an effort to reorient nature, to form it and guide it. To passively observe the growth and development of a child was to neglect the moral mission of education. Vasconcelos` strategy was classical in every sense of the word.

> I do not know why, for me, Dewey brings to mind the advantages of the rules and regulations of communities and colleges which, by giving prescribed daily obligations, the details of our corporal conduct, spare us the effort of thinking about common, trivial needs, and thus save our attention for higher problems of thought. And it is because Dewey, from what it appears, wanted to annihilate attention to matters of consequence, and set us to *inventing* each day a new way to tie our tie, to straighten our quarters.

The argument came, of course, from the Greeks: it is thanks to not having to worry about such trivialities that men can devote themselves to what is really important; in other words, the life of the *polis*. The implication of this idea, which Dewey would have rushed to point out, is that *someone* must take care of these minor tasks. In Athens, these people were, of course, women and slaves. In a democratic society, on the other hand, all citizens should participate in public life, and know how to tie their shoelaces. The sacrifice of the many should not be demanded just to finance the idleness and dilettantism of the few.

According to Vasconcelos, the child trained exclusively in the pragmatic use of his energies was only a remedial human being: "he does not know how to sit in the shade of a tree, enjoying the blessings of solitude. The gift of play lost, he cannot succeed in meditation either. Splintered by his education, disintegrated inside by the very technique that occupies his hours, he represents the exact opposite of a disciple of Socrates."[76]

In the same vein, Vasconcelos displayed a highly selective memory and a *post hoc* dramaticism when he claimed: "The importation of Dewey's system among us is an aberrant case, with consequences graver that the distribution of opium and alcohol practiced in the colonies." Dewey could produce an adapted school, "but not a free or liberating school." The duty of consciousness was not to adapt itself, but to surpass itself. Forgotten by this education was the "great literature," which, starting in childhood, awakened "the yearning for the world's superhuman values." "Why," Vasconcelos wondered, "among so much experimentation, does someone not experiment with putting a child, after he learns the ABCs, in contact with the works of Plato, or of Homer and Aeschylus, of Dante, or of Calderón and Shakespeare?"[77] School should be the "summary of the general experience of humanity," and its most important lesson, that which teaches a child to know the world that escapes necessity, and "develops according to the rules of morality or art."

Dewey's school was the result of a logical development, "but that does not make it any less sinister." Even in the United States, Vasconcelos said, Dewey's ideas could not but produce opposition in "all intelligent people." He prophesied, "In time that nation, so full of vitality, will discover how to free itself" of its consequences.[78] Vasconcelos was not entirely wrong about this. In the United States, beginning in the sixties, a revisionist movement took shape that looked with very critical eyes upon the effects of the educational revolution inspired by Dewey's ideas. In his outstanding book *Anti-Intellectualism in American Life*, published in 1962, the historian Richard Hofstadter identified progressive education as one of the factors responsible for the rampant anti-intellectualism of American society.[79]

The most important characteristic of intellectuals, Hofstadter says, is that they are people who do not live *from* ideas, but *for* ideas. Intellectual life has a spontaneous character, as well as an intrinsic determination of what is pertinent to it. There, two types of attitudes toward ideas coexist and form an equilibrium. One of them is a kind of inherited devotion to the nonsecular origin of intellectual work. This life constitutes, in some form, a religious commitment. The other is a certain playful irreverence of those who spend their time turning over ideas. Intellectual work is at once a devotional exercise and an act of freedom and imagination. The presence of both elements is fundamental. As Hofstadter says, when one's zeal for ideas, no matter how dedicated or sincere it may be, reduces them to the condition of mere instruments at the service of some preconceived end, "the intellect gets swallowed by fanaticism." If there is anything more dangerous for the life of the mind than having no independent commitment to ideas, it is precisely having an excessive commitment to just one idea. This is the characteristic of ideologues, not of intellectuals.[80] What prevents devotion from becoming fanaticism is the irreverence and the predisposition of the mind in liberty, that is to say the pleasure that intellectual activity produces, in and of itself. Irreverence is the antidote against dogmatism and rigidity. Intellectual restlessness is what makes the intellectual, in the end, one who turns answers into questions.[81] As even Hofstadter admitted, this ability has an aristocratic origin. Leisure, after all, is a privilege.

Such definition of the intellectual necessarily implies a confrontation with Dewey's pragmatism. The conflict was inevitable, although at first it might not seem so. The reason is that the school of action and Dewey's intellectual program were in themselves detrimental to the playfulness which Hofstadter thought to be crucial for a balanced intellectual life. Something of this had been perceived by Vasconcelos: "the gift of play lost, the child cannot succeed in meditation." "In the United States," Hofstadter lamented, "the play of the mind is perhaps the only form of play that is not looked upon with the most tender indulgence."[82]

However, Hofstadter's attack against new education was much more complex. According to the historian, one of the consequences was the transformation of academic programs. "The innovators," he pointed out, "had very considerable success in dismantling the old academic curriculum of high schools." After 1910, the changes were nearly revolutionary, and by the forties and fifties, the demands of those who maintained that education should be guided by the daily needs of children had become nearly insatiable.[83] Academic subjects taught in high schools fell from approximately three-quarters of the curriculum to only one-fifth. Algebra, taken in 1910 by 57 percent of American students in middle school, by 1949 had fallen to only 26 percent. The same had occurred with other subjects that traditionally had been given in schools. World history practically disappeared from the map, and learning about more recent, and useful, events replaced the study of the remote past. However, the theorists inspired by Dewey thought that there were still too many dead subjects burdening the academic programs. Geography, languages, and a whole series of "useless" lessons should completely disappear. Eliminating the remains of the feudal past of education was the mission of the revolutionaries. In order to be a useful person and a good democratic citizen, they repeated, it was not necessary to know where China or Mexico were, or to know how many emperors Rome had had, not to mention a knowledge of Latin. Mathematics, beyond basic operations of arithmetic, were useless for most students. All of this refinement was an absurd remnant of an empty encyclopedia-ism. Children should learn practical things that would be useful in their daily life as members of the community. By 1941, in American schools, not less than 274 subjects were offered, but only 59 of them could be classified as academic.[84] Thus, a kind of democratic bolshevism took American schools hostage.

This process obviously had weighty implications for the formation of elites. Teachers' energy went to the education of the slowest students and noticeably neglected the preparation of the more gifted ones. Of students enrolled in middle school, one-fifth were expected to go to college, while another fifth would go to vocational schools. The remaining three-fifths would not be capable of either of these two endeavors. Of course, the interests of the majority should guide the general direction of public education. In consequence, schools should offer an education that would be useful so that the greater part of students could adapt themselves successfully to the future that was awaiting them, a future holding nothing more than a high school diploma. Academia was thus leveled down. What kind of education would be appropriate for the majority of students, who were considered "ineducable"? Certainly, Hofstadter says, not one based on intellectual development, nor on the accumulation of knowledge, but rather another, which would consist of the practical training to be family members, consumers, and citizens. They should be taught moral and ethical values: how to conduct their home life, how to take care of their health, as well as the duties and obligations of a good citizen. Thus, schools placed the socialization of "life values" above the acquisition of knowledge. It is here that a gradual process of shunning other experiences begins. In the United States, there was the faith and the energy necessary for turning into a reality the vision of what society could be through education. The result was that the trend toward self-absorption had begun. In part, the vision of new education was plausible due to the fact that the achievements in secondary education in other countries were unknown in the United States.

Thus, in the name of usefulness, democracy, and science, many educators made unteachable children the focus of their attention, relegating the more gifted children to the margins of the system.[85] What many of Dewey's followers had done, with or without his consent, was to attack the ideas of leadership, direction, and a reflective life, which had dominated the old education, to replace it with certain notions of spontaneity, democracy, and utility. The hope was that an appropriate education, centered on the child's development, would automatically be working in favor of democracy.

The way all of this was supposed to work was quite unclear: it was thought that education should base its academic program not on the demands of society, nor on preconceived notions of what an educated person should be, but rather on the needs and interests of the child. But at the same time, it was hoped that this growth would result, spontaneously, in democracy. The democratic educator had to make schools into an experimental environment, a miniature community, the embryo of a society, where the undesirable ties of the external society would be eliminated, as much as possible.

This was a failed utopia, which was not completely surprising, since, as Hofstadter says, utopias have a peculiar tendency to short-circuit, right before the astounded eyes of their creators. Dewey, by thinking of education as growth, had established an attractive connection between the natural world and the educational process. However, this only confused and obscured the very essence of education. The metaphor of education as growth was misleading in the extreme because it confused a natural process with a social one; one which does not come about automatically, but rather deliberately, and with the active intervention of external forces. The result was that children were exalted and the problem of society was discarded because the growth of children was thought to be synonymous with health, while social traditions were the palpable manifestation of anachronistic and authoritarian chains. Dewey had thus lent his moral and intellectual authority to those who believed that curricula should be fundamentally molded based on the explicit desires of children, and that any academic content should be discontinuous from one generation to the next. "The effect of Dewey's philosophy on the design of curricular systems was," according to Hofstadter, "devastating."[86] The relativism implicit in this philosophy made any planning of the future impossible. The idea that democracy had to be the model of every social arrangement impeded the use of parameters of excellence to guide children's formation. Basically, both Dewey and his Mexican disciple, Moisés Sáenz, were excessively confident in the power of education and of schools as a socializing agent.

What is fascinating here is that Dewey was repeating an old argument against the past. The progressive school was, in this sense, part of a national epic of amnesia. For Dewey, the human experience was but a drama in which ancestral errors were to be overcome. For this reason, making the study of the past the central object of education was to neglect the present in favor of a dark past. Children had to be liberated from the past. Culture carried too many dead bodies that had to be judiciously buried so as not to disturb the present. Although Dewey knew very well that the natural impulses of children were not sufficient for achieving this emancipation, it was precisely these impulses that captured the imagination of American educators. Thus, they sought for children to be able to have a healthy distance from the past, in order to later put it to constructive use; however, in the aim of liberating education was total amnesia.

In the end, progressive education was conservative because it recognized the limitations of the masses, and condescendingly embraced the cause of the less apt, who were the greater in number. This education did not ask much of students, and of course, did not expect children to find any intrinsic pleasure in intellectual activities. Schools satisfied necessities. Thus, as Vasconcelos lamented, the intellectual dimension of play was lost. Although Dewey did not fully endorse all of these actions, his ideas were sufficiently ambiguous to make a wide interpretation possible. The educational revolution was a cross between regeneration and social experimentation. Hybrids, of yesterday and of today, have always been dangerous creatures. Often, Hofstadter would say, those who feel they should embark upon an adventure of such magnitude do not bother much with exploring the limits and dangers of their ideas. The new pedagogy indelibly marked Americans and its effects are still present.

Some analysts think that the sad state of American public education today is rooted in the experiments of the first half of the century. The dogmas of that era still impede education from being reoriented. For many, the urgent educational reform should start by asking an obvious question: What should children know? But this common sense question finds great resistance in the educational establishment of the United States. The reason is that after the revolution inspired by Dewey, to speak in those terms is nearly subversive.[87] The ideas on new pedagogy, which were innovative at the beginning of the century, ended up becoming the dominant orthodoxy. The irony is that the democratic spirit that moved progressive education had perverse, far-reaching effects. The idea that American schools, unlike those in other countries, educated not just the elite, but all citizens, is no longer true. The rampant mediocrity of the educational system has allowed social inequalities, once again, to spread and endure. In no other industrialized country is the human infrastructure in as bad a state as in the United States. Today, an analyst asserts, "other countries . . . educate the many, and we the few. To our shame, a disadvantaged child has a better chance for an equal and rigorous education, and whatever advancement it may bring, in Paris or Copenhagen than in one of our big cities."[88]

In Praise of Memory

Dewey also decisively influenced other American intellectuals who established links with Mexico. For example, the notion that ideas were instruments whose value resided in their capacity to be put to practical use inspired Frank Tannenbaum.[89] His years at Columbia exposed him to Dewey's ideas, and Dewey became his mentor. This, to a great extent, is why education was one of Tannenbaum's fields of study before he traveled to Mexico. He would dedicate his first book, *The Labor Movement*, to Dewey.[90]

Tannenbaum traveled to Mexico for the first time in 1922, to study the labor movement. Plutarco Elías Calles and Luis N. Morones influenced his first impressions of Mexico, which were, as we have seen, full of open and frank enthusiasm. It is no coincidence that the first article Tannenbaum would write about Mexico should be entitled "The Miracle School." The efforts of Vasconcelos, who was then Secretary of Education, to unite the school and the community in a pilot school undoubtedly reminded Tannenbaum of the lessons his teacher at Columbia used to give.[91] Upon his return to the United States, Tannenbaum founded the Committee of Friends of Mexico to support the model school that had inspired him so much.[92]

In 1923, Tannenbaum returned to Mexico, commissioned by the magazine *Survey*, in search of articles for a special issue that would be devoted to that country. Tannenbaum was successful in getting several Mexican intellectuals and politicians to write for the magazine. Among the collaborators were: Calles, Carrillo Puerto, Manuel Gamio, Ramón P. de Negri, José Vasconcelos, Diego Rivera, Pedro Henríquez Ureña, and Esperanza Velázquez Bringas. In this

Chapter One

issue, which would be baptized, "Mexico: A Promise," Carleton Beals, Robert Haberman, and Katherine Anne Porter also contributed.[93] Besides the well documented relationship with the labor leader Luis N. Morones, Tannenbaum established ties with Gamio, Sáenz, Luis L. León, and Miguel Othón de Mendizábal.[94] In 1926, Tannenbaum was one of those who facilitated Dewey's trip to Mexico.

Tannenbaum's political activism won him the animosity of his government, and his open sympathy for Mexico made him suspect of espionage. This was not strange because, then, all social activists were seen as undercover Bolsheviks. The FBI opened a file on Tannenbaum that remained active for thirty years. The historian sought to improve the tense relations between Mexico and the United States. In that spirit, he tried to arrange a grant for Daniel Cosío Villegas to spend time doing research at the Brookings Institution.

Tannenbaum's personal involvement with the Mexican Revolution was very deep. Faithful to his idea that the origins of the armed movement had been agrarian, he minimized the role that revolutionary intellectuals had played. Once the Revolution was over, Tannenbaum accused certain intellectuals of "trying to pattern Mexico as if it were going through some socialist revolution, or as if a syndicalist state were being built. It is neither one nor the other."[95] *Peace by Revolution*, one of Tannenbaum's most important books on Mexico, was originally conceived as a study of rural Mexican education.[96] Tannenbaum believed that it was precisely in the program of rural education, begun in the twenties, where the true spirit of the Mexican Revolution lay. The written communication between Moisés Sáenz and Tannenbaum was particularly intense, as Hale has documented, between June and November 1928.[97] *Peace by Revolution* would be dedicated to Diego Rivera.

It is no accident that Frank Tannenbaum was not just a specialized historian, but a public intellectual. This was a characteristic that he shared with his mentor, John Dewey. The existence of bridges between the two countries was intrinsically linked to the public role, above and beyond the academic role, of intellectuals. When intellectuals in the United States withdrew to their university campuses, the bridges simply collapsed. The intellectuals who had been interested in Mexico simply died out. The small extent to which the links exist today is, as we shall see, due to a few Mexican public intellectuals who have extended a precarious line of communication across the Grande River. The initiative could not arise from the overly specialized American academia. The public intellectuals who still write in the United States are a generation younger than Tannenbaum. They did not feel the fascination for the new "cultural future" that the Revolution promised for Mexico. In consequence, they have found no motive to cast a glance toward the south. A Mexican intellectual, like Carlos Fuentes, has to appear in the newspaper or on the cover of a magazine for American intellectuals to become aware of his existence. And then there is neither distance to overcome, nor a bridge to extend.

During the thirties and forties, moments of contact between the two countries were still plentiful. As Tenorio has eloquently documented, in part this exchange was due to the fact that, at that time, Mexico and the United States were facing some of the same problems.[98] One of them was "the Indian problem." In both nations native peoples were, at once, object of conscientious study and political worry. Assimilate, integrate, or preserve were the options that were being discussed in universities and governmental offices of both countries. American anthropologists traveled to Mexico to observe up close the effects of revolutionary policies. In official *indigenismo* and in the agrarian reform, they sought ideas to solve the indigenous problem of their own country.[99] An international *indigenista* movement was taking shape at that time which would allow specialists and politicians to exchange experiences and information. Manuel Gamio, Moisés Sáenz, and the American anthropologist, John Collier, formed part of that movement.

The receptiveness in those years to what was happening in other countries was notable. In Mexico, Lucio Mendieta y Núñez, editor of the journal *Revista Mexicana de Sociología* (Mexican Magazine of Sociology) and founder of the Institute of Social Investigations of the National Autonomous University of Mexico, established a relationship with the American sociologist of Russian origin, Pitirim A. Sorokin.[100] Like Tannenbaum, Sorokin was not a common academic. After having been secretary of Alexander Kerensky in Russia, Sorokin was jailed and sent into exile. In the United States, he was one of the founders of the Department of Sociology at Harvard University. Like the positivists of the nineteenth century, Sorokin aimed to find universal paradigms for explaining human behavior. However, in this search, poetry, literature, and art played an important role.[101]

Mendieta y Núñez became one of those in Mexico who were engaged in a dialogue with Sorokin. Sorokin's studies on rural sociology interested Mendieta y Núñez because they seemed to provide some kind of guide for bringing about the long-awaited incorporation of native peoples into the national community. In 1952, Sorokin received an honorary doctorate from the National Autonomous University of Mexico, upon the urging of Mendieta y Núñez. The Institute of Social Investigations published some of Sorokin's books, such as *Society, Culture and Personality* (1927), *Social Mobiliy* (1927), and *American Sex Revolution* (1956).[102]

The Shadow of Ulysses

It is inevitable that moments of greater vitality, of exposure and communion with the world should provoke reactions. In the intervals between agreement and disagreement, culture is formed. As a remedy and as an antidote, in dialogue and in opposition. Its vigor and health depend on this contact with ideas pertaining to the Other, ideas which will be appropriated, embraced, and rejected. Vasconcelos feared that all faith had been lost, that Robinson would colonize the country without opposition. With a distance, we can look with admiration upon the educational crusade begun simultaneously by reformers in Mexico and in the United States, a true war for the soul of the culture. Perhaps this retrospective admiration is for the longing of those crusaders to create a better future. Their opponents, in both countries, had to dig down into the heart of civilization to rescue the arguments and bits of wisdom that could temper this impulse toward transformation. In that struggle, there was something splendid. Something that has disappeared.

In 1932, the Mexican intellectual Ermilo Abreu Gómez scathingly criticized the cosmopolitan youth who then formed the artistic avant-garde in Mexico: "This is not an avant-garde for us, it is simply an inferior example, a feeble example of a foreign avant-garde. It is a lost and rotten branch of a tree whose roots and whose sap we cannot fully know. It is only a pitiable transplant. And as a transplant, it only produces undersized, worm-eaten, seedless fruit." Abreu wanted to organize the "genuine literary heirlooms," so that it would be the result of a Mexican legacy. The true avant-garde, Abreu preached, "is represented with humility, with sacrifice, by those writers who were able to take the pulse of our pain, and our native ability."[103]

As if the excursions to the Other were a shameful lapse, Abreu warned those who were confused: "We have to think that one day we will be held accountable: and no one will be able to raise his shoulders in a gesture of incomprehension; it will be necessary to answer with the truth of actions and intentions." Abreu was not mistaken about this. At that time the world's ideas stirred up the foundations of the national culture, for the better. The exposure in the twenties to the outside forced intellectuals to look at where they were standing. Thus, some, like Samuel Ramos and José Gorostiza, proposed a return to Mexican traditions. Others, like Jorge Cuesta, who saw cultural nationalism as the "diminishment of nationality," turned their sights to the world.[104] In attacking pariochialism and cultural nationalism, Cuesta asserted that what his foes were saying "can be expressed like this: that which is possessed has value because it is possessed; not because it is worth anything outside of its quality of being a possession; thus Mexican poverty is not less in estimation than any foreign riches; its value lies in the fact that it is ours." He wondered: "When has a Shakespeare, a Stendhal, a Baudelaire, a Dostoevski, a Conrad, been heard asking that tradition be protected, or bemoaning the disregard of men who do not rush anxiously to preserve it? Tradition is not preserved, it lives."[105]

The very polemic between nationalists and cosmopolitans is another example of the vitality of those years. Nationalists accused cosmopolitans of gracelessly imitating the Americans and the French, while cosmopolitans replied that nationalists' rejection of tradition was only a way to rid themselves of the "yardstick which makes them look smaller." The predisposition to look toward the world produced an undeniable anguish because it demanded offering reasons, not only the simple pride of origin, to justify one's culture. The more lucid ones, like Vasconcelos, stretched the spirit and took from the Greeks the certainties that they needed in order to face the challenge. But this, of course, was not a nationalistic response. It was so far from it that non-Mexicans, like Hutchins, were able to follow the same strategy. Others, in contrast, could not resist the temptation toward self-absorption, toward finding refuge in the arms of the beloved fatherland. "They are not interested," Cuesta would say of them, "in the man, but rather in the Mexican; nor in nature, but rather in Mexico; nor in history, but rather in its local anecdotes."

The path of history is strewn with nostalgic landmines. And nostalgia, as has been said, makes it difficult to use the past intelligently.[106] There is an important difference between a nostalgic remembrance and the memory of better times. Memory serves to unite the present with the past and thus find a sense of continuity. Nostalgia, on the other hand, is based on the feeling that what has gone cannot be retrieved. The nostalgic representation of the past evokes a time irredeemably lost, and, therefore, eternal and immutable. "Strictly speaking," says Christopher Lasch, "nostalgia does not entail the use of memory at all, since the past it idealizes stands outside time, frozen in unchanging perfection."[107] Although memory can also idealize what once was, it does not neglect the present. The past is a source of hope to enrich what exists now.

I titled the Spanish version of this book "The Shadow of Ulysses." I was alluding to the autobiography of Vasconcelos: *Creole Ulysses*. The name, I believe, suited an era. The mythic figure of Ulysses is a perfect metaphor for the meeting between the native and the foreign, between the past and the present. A traveler in search of a past that must be recovered in the future. Ulysses' quest does not only occur in time: his journey is made of encounters and confrontations with the strange beings who inhabit the world. It was James Joyce who was able to reconcile the everyday with the universal in his Homeric epic. Ulysses could have lived any day in any ordinary country, in the same way that the heroic times of humanity live on in our imagination. Ulysses is conjured up by travelers when their destination is uncertain, when the exotic seduces and frightens them. His memory appears here, at the place where there is both risk and opportunity. Vasconcelos' Odiseus did not appear in Mexico by accident: it was deliberately invoked.

Notes

1. Frank Tannenbaum, "Mexico—A Promise," *Survey* 1 May 1924, cited by Charles A. Hale, "Frank Tannenbaum and the Mexican Revolution," *Hispanic American Historical Review* 75, no. 2 (May 1995): 232.
2. I would like to thank María del Carmen Gastélum and Mauricio Tenorio for their generous help in the elaboration of this chapter. My argument on history and education was enriched by their work. Probably neither of them will agree completely with everything I have to say here. Responsibility for the opinions I express here is, of course, mine alone.
3. See: Helen Delpar, *The Enormous Vogue of things Mexican: Cultural Relations between the United States and Mexico 1920-1935* (Tuscaloosa, Ala.: Univ. of Alabama Press, 1992); Mauricio Tenorio Trillo, "The Cosmopolitan Mexican Summer, 1920-1949," *Latin American Research Review,* 32 (1997): 224-242.
4. Hale, "Mexican Revolution," 231.
5. Mauricio Tenorio Trillo, "Stereophonic Scientific Modernism: Social Science between Mexico and the United States, 1880-1930," *Journal of American History*, 86 (December 1999): 1156-1187. Tenorio's essay guides the first section of this chapter. (I relied on a previous version of this work: "Contrasting Social Sciences: Mexico and the U.S., 1880's/1940's. Histories of Interactive Moments," working paper, Centro de Investigación y Docencia Económicas, Mexico City, Mexico, 1994.)
6. Tenorio, "Contrasting," 45. On this subject, see Ricardo Godoy, "Franz Boas and His Plans for an International School of American Archeology and Ethnology in Mexico," *Journal of the History of the Behavioral Sciences*, 13 (1977): 228-242.
7. On Gamio, see Carmen Ruiz, *Gamio: arqueología y nación* (San Cristóbal, Mexico: Instituto Chiapaneco de Cultura, 1993).
8. Tenorio, "Contrasting," 47.
9. Tenorio, "Contrasting," 47.
10. Tenorio, "Stereophonic," 1179.
11. Tenorio, "Contrasting," 66.
12. "Profiles: John Dewey," *Prospects* 13, no. 3 (1983). On Dewey, see for example, Robert B. Westbrook, *John Dewey and American Democracy* (Ithaca, N.Y.: Cornell Univ. Press, 1991).
13. John A. Britton, "Moisés Sáenz: Nacionalista Mexicano," *Historia Mexicana*, 22 (July-Sept. 1972): 78-79.
14. Josefina Vázquez de Knauth, *Nacionalismo y Educación en México* (Mexico: El Colegio de México, 1975), 160.
15. Enrique Krauze, "La Escuela Callista," in E. Krauze, J. Meyer, and C. Reyes, *Historia de la Revolución Mexicana, 1924-1928: La Reconstrucción Económica* (Mexico: El Colegio de México, 1977), 295-321.
16. Mary Kay Vaughan, *Cultural Politics in Revolutionary Teachers, Peasants and Schools in Mexico, 1930-1946* (Tucson: Univ. of Arizona Press, 1997); Mary Kay Vaughan, "Ideological Changes in Mexican Educational Policy, Programs and Texts (1920-1940)," in *Los Intelectuales y el Poder en México,* eds. R. A. Camp, C. A. Hale, and J. Z. Vázquez (Mexico: El Colegio de México; Los Angeles: UCLA, 1991), 509.

17. Krauze, "La Escuela Callista," 297.

18. Moisés Sáenz, "Algunos Aspectos de la Educación en México," extract from the speech that professor Moisés Sáenz, Assistant Secretary of Public Education (Subsecretario de Educación Pública), gave at the State of Texas Teachers' Convention in Dallas, Texas, November 1925, *La Casa de Pueblo y el Maestro Rural Mexicano*, ed. Engracia Loyo Bravo (Mexico: Secretaria de Educación Pública/Caballito, 1985), 23.

19. José Vasconcelos (1882-1959) was one of the most important figures in the postrevolutionary scene in Mexico. He was both an intellectual and a politician. He served under president Álvaro Obregón as minister of Education and as president of the National University in the 1920s. As an ideologue, he was an adamant supporter of racial intermixing. While the idea was not new, Vasconcelos coined the concept of the "Cosmic race." A prolific writer, he parted ways with the revolutionary leaders of Mexico in 1929, when he ran as an independent presidential candidate against the official nominee. After his failure at the polls, Vasconcelos became increasingly embittered and he gravitated to the far right of the spectrum of politics.

20. Krauze, "La Escuela Callista," 299.

21. Eulalia Guzmán, "La Cultura," in *La Escuela Nueva o de la Acción* 1923, cited in Claude Fell, *José Vasconcelos: Los años del águila (1920-1925)* (Mexico: UNAM, 1989), 150. It is not completely clear whether it was Vasconcelos or Félix Palaviccini who sent Guzmán to study educational systems in the United States.

22. I am grateful to María del Carmen Gastélum for having pointed out to me this change in Vasconcelos' attitude.

23. Vasconcelos, "Observaciones al Reglamento de la SEP," *Boletín de la SEP*, (September 1992), cited by Fell, *José Vasconcelos*, 149.

24. Fell, *José Vasconcelos*, 150.

25. In 1909 several independent Mexican intellectuals, including Vasconcelos, Isidro Fabela, Alfonso Reyes, together with occasional foreigners like Pedro Henríquez Ureña, founded a scholarly discussion club known as the Ateneo de la Juventud. The Ateneo, which met regularly in Mexico City, consisted of students, writers, artists, professionals, and teachers committed to free intellectual inquiry and a search for new intellectual concepts to replace the "scientism" and "dogmatism" of prerevolutionary positivism. Dewey's pragmatism and his faith in science was inimical to the philosophical approach of the *Ateneo* circle. These intellectuals did not believe in science but in the metaphysical power of the spirit. See: James D. Cockcroft, *Intellectual Precursors of the Mexican Revolution, 1900-1913* (Austin: Univ. of Texas Press, 1976), 58.

26. Antonio Caso (1883-1943) was one of the most prominent members of the Ateneo de la Juventud circle.

27. Antonio Caso, "Las Escuelas de Primera Enseñanza," *El Universal Ilustrado*, 27 July 1917, cited by Fell, *José Vasconcelos*, 163.

28. Fell, *José Vasconcelos*, 158.

29. Tenorio, "Contrasting," 67.

30. See: John Dewey, *Impressions of Soviet Russia and the Revolutionary World, Mexico, China, Turkey, 1929*, ed. William W. Brickman (New York: Columbia Univ. Press, 1964); James T. Farrel, "Dewey in Mexico," in Sidney Hook, *John Dewey: Philosopher of Science and Freedom* (New York: Barnes & Noble, 1950).

31. Dewey, *John Dewey's Impressions,* 133-141, 69.

32. Tenorio, "Constrasting," 70.

33. John Gunnel, *The Descent of Political Theory: The Genealogy of an American Vocation* (Chicago: Univ. of Chicago Press, 1993), 143.

34. Gunnel, *The Descent of Political Theory,* 143.

35. John Dewey, in the introduction of Elsie Ripley Clapp, *The Use of Resources in Education* (New York: n.p., 1952), in *Education in the United States: A Documentary History* 5, ed. Sol Cohen (Los Angeles: Univ. of California Press, 1974), 3128-3129.

36. See below.

37. See Enrique Krauze, "Pasión y Contemplación en Vasconcelos, I," *Vuelta,* 7 (May 1983).

38. John Dewey, *The Public and Its Problems* (New York: Henry Holt, 1927).

39. T. V. Smith, *The Democratic Way of Life* (Chicago: Univ. of Chicago Press, 1926).

40. James D. Cockcroft, *Outlaws in the Promised Land: Mexican Immigrant Workers and America's Future* (New York: Grove Press, 1986), 39, 259.

41. Christopher Domínguez, "José Vasconcelos, Padre de los Bastardos," in *Tiros en el concierto. Literatura mexicana del siglo V* (Mexico: ERA, 1997), 95-98.

42. José Vasconcelos and Manuel Gamio, *Aspects of Mexican Civilization. (Lectures on the Harris Foundation, 1926)* (Chicago: Univ. of Chicago Press, 1926). I would like to thank Luis Barrón for having provided me with these and other texts.

43. The texts published by Vasconcelos in Chicago have not received much attention by historians. For more information, see José Joaquín Blanco, *Se llamaba Vasconcelos. Una Evocación Crítica* (Mexico: Fondo de Cultura Económica, 1971). For example, Hernández Busto mentioned this speech, but cites it incorrectly. Ernesto Hernández Busto, *Perfil Derecho: Siete Escritores de Entreguerras* (México: Aldus, 1996), 145-167.

44. Vasconcelos, "Latin American Basis," 4-5.

45. Vasconcelos, "Latin American Basis," 4-5, 19. "In the manner of enjoying life— there is where the thinker should search; where the artist should discover those traits that enable him to portray the soul of a nation or a period."

46. Vasconcelos, "Latin American Basis," 20-21.

47. Vasconcelos, "Latin American Basis," 20-21

48. Vasconcelos, "Latin American Basis," 35.

49. Vasconcelos, as already stated, contended for the presidency in that year.

50. Vasconcelos, "Latin American Basis," 55.

51. Vasconcelos, "Latin American Basis," 80.

52. Vasconcelos, "Latin American Basis," 85.

53. John Dewey, *Liberalism and Social Action* (New York: Putnam's, 1938), 72-73.

54. Vasconcelos, "Latin American Basis," 96. "If all nations then build theories to justify their policies or to strengthen their deeds, let us develop in Mexico our own theories; or at least let us be certain, that we choose among the foreign theories of thought those that stimulate our growth instead of those that restrain it."

55. Vasconcelos, "Latin American Basis," 99.

56. José Vasconcelos, "A Mexican's Point of View," in J. Rippy, J. Vasconcelos, and G. Stevens, *American Policies Abroad, Mexico* (Chicago: Univ. of Chicago Press, 1928), 103-143.

57. Vasconcelos, "A Mexican's Point of View," 104-105.

58. See below.

59. José Vasconcelos, *Boletín de la Universidad*, 1 (September 1922): 179, cited by Engracia Loyo, "Lectura Para el Pueblo, 1921-1940," in *La Educación en la Historia de México*, ed. Josefina Zoraida Vázquez (Mexico: El Colegio de México, 1922), 150.

60. Loyo, "Lectura," 249.

61. Fell, *José Vasconcelos*, 485-486.

62. José Vasconcelos, "Los Cien Libros," Gómez Morín Archive, 284:1306, Instituto Tecnológico Autónomo de México. Mexico City: n.d. I thank Javier Garcíadiego for bringing this article to my attention.

63. Vasconcelos' idiosyncratic list of the hundred essential books and authors read as follows: Homer, Sophocles, Euripides, five dialogues of Plato (*Apology, Phedo, Phadeo, Thimeo*, and the *Republic*), the *Organum* of Aristotle, the *Golden Verses* by Pithagoras, Geometry, by Euclid, *The Greek History* by Thucidides, *History of Greek Literature*, by Murray, seven books from the Bible (the Four Gospels, the Apocalypse, Saint Paul's Epistle), *Roman History*, by Mommsen, a modern book on Geology, the *World History*, by Ricet, Astronomy with Copernicus' system, *The Mechanic of Newton*, the *Divine Comedy* by Dante, the *Small Flowers* by Saint Francis and his biography by Celan, the *Imitation* by Kempis, an abridged version of Thomas Aquinas' works, for instance, Gilson's, the *Thousand and One Nights*, *La Chanson* by Roland, *Don Quijote* by Cervantes, five plays by Lope de Vega, five plays by Calderón de la Barca, five plays by Shakespeare, *Mount Carmelo*, by St. John of the Cross, *Las Moradas* by St. Therese, the *Louisads* by Camoens, Bernal Díaz del Castillo's account of the *Conquista* as well as the *Letters* by Hernán Cortés, five novels by Balzac, five novels by Dostoievsky, Goethe's *Faustus*, *The History of Spanish America* by Carlos Pereyra, *History of Ancient Philosophy* by Mondolfe, *Modern Philosophy* by Whitehead, *Political Economy* by Somabart, a summary of Marx, *History of Materialism* by Lange, *Psychology* by Janot, *Levels of Knowledge* by Maritain, *Immediate Facts of Conscience* by Bergson, five Spanish American novels: *Facundo, Doña Bárbara, El Périquillo Sarniento, Ifigenia* by Teresa de la Parra, *Las Lanzas Coloradas* by Uslar Pietri, poetry by Edgar Allan Poe, Walt Whitman, Rubén Darío, an anthology of Mexican Poets, *History of Mexico* by Bravo Ugarte, etc. Vasconcelos' philosophical leanings, education, and prejudices are all evident in this list of authors.

64. Moisés Sáenz, *Carapan: Bosquejo de una Experiencia* (Lima: n.p., 1936).

65. The vision of the minority that has historically opposed progress in the United States is well documented by Lasch. Christopher Lasch, *The True and Only Heaven. Progress and Its Critics* (New York: Norton, 1991).

66. Instituto Nacional de Estadística, Geografía e Informática (INEGI), *Estadísticas Históricas de México*, 1 (Mexico: INEGI, 1944), 44-107.

67. Thomas D. Snyder, ed. *120 Years of American Education: A Statistical Portrait* (Washington: National Center for Educational Statistics, 1993), 7-11.

68. Snyder, *120 Years of American Education*, 155.

69. John Dewey, "The Primary Education Fetich," *Forum*, 25 (1898): 315-317, reproduced in Cohen, *Education*, 2217.

70. Dewey, "The Primary Education Fetich," 2218.

71. Sáenz, *Carapan*, 22.

72. Sáenz, *Carapan,* 29.

73. José Vasconcelos, "De Robinson a Odiseo. Pedagogía Estructurativa," in *Antología de Textos Sobre Educación,* ed. Alicia Molina (Mexico: Fondo de Cultura Económica, 1981), 33.

74. José Enrique Rodó, *Obras Selectas* (Buenos Aires: El Ateneo, 1964). *Ariel* (1900), was an antiutilitarian plea. On the transformations of the intellectual ideal embodied in Ariel, see François Bourricaud, "The Adventures of Ariel," *Daedalus,* 101 (summer 1972): 109-136 and Domínguez, "José Vasconcelos," 47-195.

75. Vasconcelos, "De Robinson," 33.

76. Vasconcelos, "De Robinson," 44-45.

77. Vasconcelos, "De Robinson," 52.

78. Vasconcelos, "De Robinson," 45-46.

79. Richard Hofstadter, *Anti-Intellectualism in American Life* (New York: Vintage Books, 1963).

80. Hofstadter, *Anti-Intellectualism in American Life,* 27-29.

81. Hofstadter, *Anti-Intellectualism in American Life,* 30.

82. Hofstadter, *Anti-Intellectualism in American Life,* 33.

83. Hofstadter, *Anti-Intellectualism in American Life,* 341.

84. Hofstadter, *Anti-Intellectualism in American Life,* 342.

85. Hofstadter, *Anti-Intellectualism in American Life,* 353.

86. Hofstadter, *Anti-Intellectualism in American Life,* 377.

87. Paul Gagnon, "What Should Children Know?" *Atlantic Monthly,* 276 (December 1995).

88. Gagnon, "What Should Children Know?," 67.

89. Hale, "Frank Tannenbaum," 226.

90. Frank Tannenbaum, *The Labor Movement: Its Conservative Functions and Social Consequences* (New York: G.P. Putnam Sons, 1921).

91. Frank Tannenbaum, "The Miracle School," *Century Magazine,* no. 106 (August 1923): 499-506.

92. Hale, "Frank Tannenbaum," 231.

93. "Mexico—A Promise," *Survey,* 1 May 1924.

94. Hale, "Frank Tannenbaum," 237.

95. Hale, "Frank Tannenbaum," 240.

96. Frank Tannenbaum, *Peace by Revolution: An Interpretation of Mexico* (New York: Columbia Univ. Press, 1933).

97. Hale, "Frank Tannenbaum," 244.

98. Tenorio, "Constrasting," 72.

99. Tenorio, "Constrasting," 73.

100. Tenorio, "Constrasting," 74-79.

101. Tenorio, "Constrasting," 74-79.

102. Tenorio, "Constrasting," 74-79.

103. Ermilo Abreu Gómez, "¿Existe una Crisis en Nuestra Literatura de Vanguardia?," *El Ilustrado* (April 1932), reproduced in Gerardo de la Concha, *La Razón y la Afrenta: Antología del Panfleto y la Polémica en México* (Toluca, Mex.: Instituto Mexiquense de Cultura, 1995), 461-468.

104. On the polemic between nationalists and cosmopolitans in Mexico, see: Guillermo

Sheridan, *México en 1932: La polémica nacionalista* (Mexico: Fondo de Cultura Económica, 1999). On the *Contemporáneos* generartion, to which Cuesta belonged, see: Guillermo Sheridan, *Los Contemporáneos ayer* (México: Fondo de Cultura Económica, 1993), 390-394.

105. Jorge Cuesta, "La Literatura y el Nacionalismo," in Jorge Cuesta, *Poemas y Ensayos* (Mexico: UNAM, 1973), reproduced in Concha, *La Razón,* 469-470.

106. Lasch, *The True and Only,* 82.

107. Lasch, *The True and Only,* 83.

Chapter 2

Paper Tigers

When a society decays,
the first thing to be infected with gangrene is the language.
Octavio Paz[1]

If we could climb a hill to observe the horizon of intellectual life in Mexico and the United States, we would see two paths that never meet, but that advance in a parallel direction. In the distance, we might perceive a few old crossing stations, now nearly forgotten.[2] We might notice that the last few miles in both paths are full of potholes. Why? Several processes seem to have co-occurred in the two countries. In Mexico and in the United States, public discussion has become impoverished. Mexican and American intellectuals, as creators and transmitters of culture, seem to have entered a process of decadence that can be appreciated in by comparing between generations. It seems that in the latter half of the century a stage of national self-absorption began. And finally, coupled with the erosion of intellectual life in both countries, there has been a marked deterioration in general education. This should come as no surprise. As we have seen, in both Mexico and the United States, education's finest hour was also the finest hour for intellectuals. In the past, it was precisely in the field of education that the battles for the soul of the culture were fought. None of this is a coincidence.

Parallel Histories

In his prologue to *Animal Farm*, George Orwell wrote that if freedom means anything it is the right to tell others what they do not want to hear.[3] An author who has exercised this right with particular vigor in recent years is American historian Russell Jacoby. In his book *The Last Intellectuals*, published in 1987, Jacoby explored a singular void in the United States: young public intellectuals.[4] Public intellectuals are those who address an audience that is both and educated, in nonspecialized language and on topics of general interest.

Why has a generation of public intellectuals failed to appear in the United States? Jacoby's book attempts to explain this. While the causes of this phenomenon are not readily apparent, its consequence is obvious: the impoverishment of public culture. The youngest intellectuals no longer need or want a broader audience because they are almost exclusively professors. Their home is the university campus, their audience is their circle of colleagues and their vehicle of expression are the specialized journals that publish their papers. Unlike intellectuals in the past, whose vocation was more general in its application, younger ones have settled into specialized fields and disciplines. And for good reason: their jobs, promotions, and salaries depend exclusively on evaluation by other specialists. This dependence affects both the subjects they take on, and the language they employ. Independent intellectuals who write for the well-educated, but nonspecialized reader are becoming extinct.[5] Even the natural habitat of intellectuals who are not professors is disappearing: American cities have undergone a radical transformation in the last thirty years. The middle class has escaped to the suburbs and the old urban centers have become slums. Industrial development and the decadence of cities have done away with Bohemia, as well as the places where intellectuals traditionally met to think about issues and discuss issues. Intellectuals from the era prior to "academia" could communicate with a wider following of readers; they mastered the language of public discourse and were vigorous writers. In contrast, although the new academics surpass the old intellectuals in number, almost no one outside of academic circles has heard of them. Their vernacular is a specialized jargon, incomprehensible to the ordinary reader. American professors inhabit insulated societies and speak a cryptic language that only the initiated understand. When intellectuals became academics, they no longer needed to use public prose in their writing. Thus, they have stopped doing so, and now have entirely forgotten what public prose was. Today, cultural life in the United States is dependent upon an ever smaller number of older intellectuals who have no successors. The younger intellectuals are busy, concerned with advancing their academic careers. While professional life flourishes on campus, public culture is aging and becoming ever more impoverished.

The generation gap, Jacoby points out, is marked by a profound irony. The intellectuals who are *not* in the public arena are the very ones who came of age in the sixties. Those were the years of the counterculture, of protests and dissatisfaction with the establishment. Fifteen years of political and cultural ferment. But, in the end, it was all nothing more than fermentation, as it produced no beer, no wine, nor any other brew or spirit that might have resulted from the agitation and hope of those years. For this judgment to come from a leftist intellectual, of all people, is no doubt revealing. "How is it possible that these veterans of movements, who often targeted the university, derided their teachers, and ridiculed past thinkers could mature into such earnest professionals, quieter than older intellectuals?"[6]

After the dust raised by the commotion of the sixties had settled, it became clear that many young intellectuals had never left school; many of that generation realized that there was nowhere else to go. In consequence, they became radical sociologists, Marxist historians, and feminist theorists, but not public intellectuals.

American universities succeeded in greedily swallowing up intellectuals, who would not come to inhabit the public arena, because the number of professors had grown disproportionately. Between 1920 and 1970, the population of the United States doubled, but the number of academics increased tenfold: from 50,000 in 1920 to 500,000 in 1970. With few exceptions, Jacoby asserts, by the late fifties intellectuals had abandoned the cities to populate university campuses: they exchanged cafés for cafeterias.[7] University jobs allowed them to go from a life of uncertainty and economic straits to one more comfortable, stable, and predictable. The cost of all this, which was not evident at the time, would be the separation of intellectuals from their audience. Intellectuals began to seek the approval of their colleagues, and not their readers. As Jacoby points out, the deformation and corruption of academic life are by no means new; what is new is the magnitude of the phenomenon. "When universities occupied a quadrant of cultural life, their ills (and virtues) meant one thing. When they staked out the turf, their rules became *the* rules."[8] Therefore, the books that academics write place the data, arguments, findings, and conclusions first: the text itself is the least important element. Literary style has become irrelevant: substance, not form, is what matters.

Thus, the mystery of the disappearance of intellectuals is unraveled. By the time the generation born in the forties came of age, the migration of intellectuals to universities was nearly complete. The intellectual = professor equation had already become well-established. The generation of young people headed for the universities and there the would-be intellectuals stayed. The opportunity to master public prose never presented itself. In spite of there being literally hundreds of thousands of them, professors are invisible to the society as a whole. And leaving the university is not an option: outside of the campus, there is nowhere to go. In the era of academia, to make a living "selling reviews and articles stopped being difficult, it became impossible." The choice is between acclimating to the university or resigning oneself to the bleak landscape beyond it. As a result, the sixties generation never managed to establish a lasting public presence. Like the flowers they took to their demonstrations, the future intellectuals soon withered before they could even begin

to blossom. Some became insurance salesmen; they bought houses in the suburbs. Others got lost in the winding paths of academia. Almost none survived.
Only conservative intellectuals remained suspicious of academia. Some of them
criticized professionalization. It should come as no surprise that they have
loomed large in the culture wars.

Since 1987, some encouraging developments have emerged. A few professors, against all odds, have taken to the fore. Philosophers, such as Richard
Rorty, Michael Walzer, Jean Bethke Elshtain, Michael Sandel, and Martha
Nussbaum have tried to invigorate a public philosophy. They are following John
Dewey's trail. Other academics are also trying to overcome seminar rooms to
reach out to a larger audience. However, it is not yet clear if they will be successful. One thing is certain: they are swimming against the current. Also, in the
last decade the appearance of black intellectuals has generated much attention.
These new African American public intellectuals are singular in many respects.
For one, their concerns seem somehow narrower than those of previous generations of American intellectuals. While people such as Cornell West, Henry
Louis Gates, and Stephen Carter often write on culture, law, and politics, much
of their work is centered on race and race relations. Their undeniable successes
show, however, that a literate public still exists. Finally, science writers have
managed to capture the imagination of many readers. As Jacoby himself ac-
knowledges in a new preface to *The Last Intellectuals,* "a group of science
writers has more or less filled the space vacated by humanists." Authors such
as Stephen Gould, Oliver Sacks, Jared Diamond, Jonathan Weiner, and Jeremy
Bernstein are writing with clarity on matters of wide intellectual interest. Yet,
in spite of all these signs, the main hypothesis of *The Last Intellectuals* seems
to hold. The economic incentives that turned public intellectuals into specialized professors have not subsided. Only time will tell if this pessimism was
exaggerated.

At first glance, what happens in the United States would have little to do
with intellectual life in Mexico. There, there was no "lost generation," and
public intellectuals abound. There are no ravenous college campuses waiting to
devour late-night poets, and bohemia has not disappeared. Mexico City, a
country unto itself, offers the perfect urban habitat for intellectual gatherings
and other forms of informal contact to flourish. If anything, the city has absorbed the suburbs, and intellectuals are not nobodies in society; on the contrary, they enjoy a prestige and influence unheard of in other countries. In
short, a paradise for the *literati.* The image, however, is deceiving.

When examined closely, circumstances in Mexico are not so different. Public
intellectuals have not disappeared, but they have become impoverished: compared to their predecessors, the role played by Mexican intellectuals today is
a poor one. Public debate has deteriorated in the last forty years. There is also a
generational similarity. In Mexico, too, the sixties produced a critical moment:

the student movement. Like the sixties in the United States, the movement of 1968 and its generation took on mythical proportions. In the political imagination there would henceforth be a "Before October 2" and an "After October 2," the date on which the Mexican army massacred students in Tlatelolco Plaza.[9] The event became an identity marker for those who participated in the movement and a distance marker in the historical memory of the country. "In a few short months," remembers Enrique Krauze, one of the most prominent members of that generation, "the sanctity of the Mexican State was turned asunder and the creativity of civil society appeared."[10]

The year 1968 would produce palpable evidence of the changes that the country had been silently undergoing for decades: the expansion of the middle class, the end of the Mexican economic miracle, and the incapacity of the authoritarian regime to transform itself democratically and channel the political participation of new social actors. The political, social, and intellectual energy of the movement of 1968 was formidable. On the twenty-fifth anniversary of the events of that year, Krauze wrote:

It has become fashionable to reduce that juncture in our history to a sort of generational myth. For me, and for many other young people of the time, that experience meant above all a sense of liberation. Marching freely along the streets of the city: occupying physical, visual, auditory spaces in it, listening to debates, news programs and songs of liberty on the University Radio; reinventing our own the French Assembly at street-corners, cafés, or auditoriums; in the marches and in the protests feeling the joy of spontaneous solidarity; shouting *"viva!"* in the University esplanade on the afternoon of Mexican Independence Day, not with the President of the Republic, but instead with Herberto Castillo[11]; in essence, repudiating, with a short, collective "no," a political system we intuitively knew to be oppressive, antiquated, destructive, these were the many facets of the same festival of freedom that would soon be drowned out by the Tlatelolco massacre.[12]

One member of that generation, Luis González de Alba, was to give the most lucid and deeply felt testimony of the 1968 movement.[13]

And despite all this, what was the intellectual outcome of that explosion of vitality, of that "festival of freedom"? The cloud of dust was of such magnitude that it has taken nearly three decades to settle. Today, we can look back with some clarity. The 1968 movement produced nothing comparable to the expectations it created. The generation has excelled in literature, not in political analysis. Its finest moments have occurred in fiction, not in reality. There is not a void, as there is in the United States, but something is missing.

Perhaps it is because intellectual life contains unexplicit similarities between the two countries over the last thirty years that Jacoby's argument is so fascinating for some Mexicans. The comparisons are not far-fetched and some have already been put to the test. "Where," Roger Bartra asks, "are the Mexican bohemia and pseudo-bohemia headed?" They take refuge in politicized, governmentally run, bureaucratic universities, where subsidies, salaries, curriculums, sabbaticals, degrees, and offices reign: a universe that is completely foreign and adverse to free and independent intellectual creation.[14] For Bartra:

> Somehow, in the United States, we can see the reflection of some of our possible futures. There the era of professionalization has gone on for several years and passed through various stages. The academic paradise in the United States has come to what seems to be a dead-end street.

In Mexico, what is the nature of the readership that intellectuals still have? "Mainly the hated masses in the universities and the uncomfortable philanthropic ogres of the government. If the first has fragmented itself into little towers of bored, specialized excellence, and the second are becoming technocratic dinosaurs, we can imagine a sinister and gray future for intellectuals."[15]

However, the conquest of the university as a space for critical debate was considered by intellectuals of the generation of 1968 as one of their great triumphs. "In the years following the repression," says Carlos Monsiváis,

> the former security that had installed itself once again in the cultural sector found itself suspended and finally liquidated by what was occurring in universities. There, in spite of all the currying of favor and the corruption, the nucleus of critical thinking and resistance continued and spread. Its enormous and growing importance is a fact, in spite of the proclivity to travel along the Great Ideological Highways. . . . What the sixties had left was an atmosphere full of faith in the potential of intellectual and artistic work.[16]

The confidence reflected a social process taking place. In the late sixties and the early seventies, Mexican intellectuals acquired something they had never had before: a grassroots base. Only, it was not made up of laborers or *campesinos,* but rather of students. In Latin America, the sixties "were marked by the access of millions of lower-middle class youths to higher public education that decisively shaped their lives and their countries."[17] According to Castañeda, the increase in university enrollment between 1960 and 1980 can hardly be exaggerated. In Mexico, it increased fifteenfold: from 76,000 students in 1960, to 247,00 in 1970 and to 1.3 million in 1987.[18] In the rest of Latin America, the gross rate of students in higher education was 6.3 percent in 1970, 11.7 percent in 1975, 13.5 percent in 1980, and 16.6 percent in 1985.[19] A perhaps unintentional consequence of this process was that universities became hotbeds of radical political activism.

Although in the United States the process of university expansion was more inclusive and general than in Mexico, the effects of this process were significant in both countries. As Castañeda points out, many Latin American nations were not prepared for the extraordinary expansion of universities:

> Teachers were ill prepared or unavailable; secondary and even elementary education remained deficient at best; jobs did not exist and would not be accessible if and when the exploding student bodies graduated: The ensuing politicization that shook many universities was unavoidable as centers of higher education became stakes in political games. These accorded scant priority to training but constituted inevitable by-products of the rapid extension of higher education to new sectors of society.[20]

In a way, what happened to the left in the universities of the United States and Mexico was not so different. A sort of shift took place. The real world was replaced by a fictitious one. Social criticism became a vicarious endeavor. The most important serious deformation in both countries was that the perception intellectuals had of society was distorted. The result of this confusion, a particular form of diversion, was that social criticism became, at best, sterile. The obvious was ignored: students were not the oppressed masses of the country, and the revolution would not come about in the classroom. The self-deception is binational.

C. Wright Mills: The Last Connection

The intellectuals of the generation of 1968 (just like their American contemporaries) were "readers and friends of C. Wright Mills," and thought that the mission of the intellectual was to be a revolutionary avant-garde. Like Dewey, three decades earlier, Mills visited the National Autonomous University of Mexico, in 1960. Perhaps that was the last moment of shared intelligence between Mexican and American intellectuals.

According to Krauze, "Mills envied the potential influence of the Latin American intellectual, whom he held to be the only factor that could bring about transformation in under-developed countries." Fuentes dedicated his second novel, *The Death of Artemio Cruz*, to Mills. Enrique González Pedrero and Julieta Campos translated *Listen, Yankee: the Revolution in Cuba* (1960) for the publishing house Fund for Economic Culture (Fondo de Cultura Económica). González Pedrero personally met the American sociologist, who taught a seminar in Mexico on Marxism. Mills lectured at the Institute of Social Research (Instituto de Investigaciones Sociales), which Pablo González Casanova directed. González Pedrero remembers:

After each session, we used to chat with Wright Mills, a very simple, hardworking man, a highly cultivated democrat. . . . Pablo González Casanova, Carlos Fuentes and I became good friends of Wright Mills. This explains why he dedicated his book, *The Marxists* (1962) to us, which, by the way, was not published by the Fund, but rather by the publishing house Era, in 1964.[21]

Of all the personalities involved, the youngest was González Pedrero (b. 1930), who was then barely thirty years old. Pablo González Casanova (b. 1922) and Carlos Fuentes (b.1928) were, respectively, thirty-eight and thirty-two years old. C. Wright Mills (b. 1916) was forty-four: not much older than his Mexican companions. Mills died shortly afterwards, at the age of 46. The three Mexicans who survive him are approaching, or have already passed, their seventieth birthday. They are survivors of a bygone era. They are also the last generational step in a truncated ladder. Their testimonies are remnants of a fallen bridge.[22] Later, American anthropologist Oscar Lewis was declared *persona non grata* for having written a study on urban poverty in Mexico: *Los hijos de Sánchez* (1961). The nationalist *Sociedad Mexicana de Geografía* filed a lawsuit against the book, since Mexican "patriots" resented the study as an "insult."

Mills' influence on the Mexican left would be deplored by conservative intellectuals on both sides of the border. In the eighties, his replacement would be the linguist Noam Chomsky. The magazine *Vuelta* had tried to inoculate the Mexican intellectual world against the fashionable trends of multiculturalism and political correctness, publishing essays by Daniel Bell, John Searle, and others. Although the echoes of the culture wars being waged in the United States were remote, the Mexican magazine translated articles criticizing academic radicalism and defending the cannon of Western studies. However, the allegations made were barely intelligible to the uninitiated.

In the United States, Mills' spirit, language, and example indelibly marked the young New Left.[23] For the intellectuals of this stream of thought, Mills was a figure of heroic proportions. However, his successors became sociologists, not public intellectuals. There, as in Mexico, university politics replaced true politics. South of the Rio Grande, it is true, academic salaries were not high enough to attract the interest of a great number of intellectuals. But if the comfortable effects of professionalization were not felt in quite the same way in Mexico, the diversion of academic life was indeed comparable. In both countries, professors became campus revolutionaries. Others threw themselves into the task of organizing urban and rural guerrillas. The most famous of these is Sebastián Guillén, whose alias, Subcommander Marcos, is a household name.

American left-wing academics live in the clouds; they have taken unintelligible academic jargon to be synonymous with profundity. The conflicts of academia, the culture wars, postmodernism, poststructuralism, all are caricatures of real-world conflicts. It is the Great Diversion, which in many aspects resembles the radical never-never land of the Great Highways, which seduced so many Mexicans both in and out of the universities. In the United States, revolutionaries now find their inspiration in Derrida and Foucault, and devote themselves to the enthusiastic pursuit of the subversion of language. Clarity in their writing style is, of course, anathema. They dream that their jargon will defeat capitalism as they drink coffee in the professor's lounge and collect their paycheck every fortnight. And with all this, academics conceive of themselves as the revolutionary avant-garde. Their task is to erode from within the oppressive worldview of their students. As Jacoby acidly asserts, their cubicles are the new trenches, their research tools are the new weapons, and the professors of literature are the new avant-garde revolutionaries.[24] The magnitude of this collective illusion is hard to exaggerate. "While liberals and conservatives debate over the merits of an allegedly 'Eurocentric' curriculum, policies designed to promote racial diversity and 'sensitivity' and the theoretical implications of poststructuralism," the fundamental issues go unnoticed.[25] Subversion here is a joke.

In Mexico, the boom of the university not only allowed revolution to be confined to the chalkboard, as in the United States, but it also encouraged a characteristic self-absorption. The "teachings, writings and sermons on dependency theory" provided a discourse appropriate to the cause of academic independence.[26] Dependency theory was, after all, a social theory that had originated in Latin America. The novels of the Latin American Boom validated a sense of cultural pride. The Nueva Trova Cubana became the anthem of emancipation: "the singers and musicians found words and rhythms that were both recognizable and authentically Latin American, finally reversing the import syndrome of the past." A world our own had been created. "The students purchased books on a unprecedented scale, while the authors discarded any doubts or insecurities since their wisdom was ratified by the truest of measuring rods: a mass following in an ancestrally elitist environment."[27] There was also the possibility of an Authentically Popular Culture to counterbalance High Culture. For Monsiváis, this highbrow culture "has only been achieved and embodied among us in a very precarious and irregular way. What has been common have been poor imitations, irrational devotion, the colonized spirit as the unrestricted and superficial acceptation of everything that comes from a metropolis."[28] Ermilo Abreu would have clapped his hands with enthusiasm: High Culture was nothing but a "pitiful transplant." Unlike in the thirties, now it was possible to take pride in the national glories. Certainly the world was recognizing Latin American vigor and originality. In the United States, according to Jacoby, the prominence that Latin American novels enjoyed was another example of the fact that "the creative juices flow on the outside, the margins, as malls and campuses cement over the center."[29] Latin America's moment of glory gave cultural nationalism consistency. The prominence of regional topics also obscured the fact that being linked to the outside world not only involved dependence on the metropoles, but also dialogue and participation. Cultural self-affirmation thus created gave rise to a sense of self-sufficiency. This world made of images and symbols was vast enough to make it unnecessary to go beyond it just yet. The insularity thus created would become evident in the decades to come.

The habitat of the generation of 1968 was the Latin American Island, and their drink was the nectar of compensatory pride. There was not split with the outside world because the outside world had been relegated to the realm of the other. The net result was an impoverishment of perspectives: the continued vigor of cultural movements depends critically on their contact with the outside world. Even the literary heroes of the Boom belonged to a previous generation and had spent many years of their life in Europe, as was the case, for example, of Julio Cortázar. For their successors, however, the horizon narrowed.

There are other reasons, also, that explain the intellectual impoverishment experienced by Mexico. It must be stated explicitly that this proposition does not apply to anyone in particular. The intellectuals of 1968 are not less lucid or brilliant than their predecessors. This is not a judgment on anyone's integrity or genius. On the contrary, complex impersonal factors influence the formation of a generation. These factors also explain some of the vitality of the culture. Three processes, besides the expansion of the university system, seem to be relevant in the case of Mexico. The first has to do with the consolidation of the postrevolutionary political regime. By the late seventies, it had been quite some time since the institutional construction of the country had been concluded. Intellectuals belonging to the generation of 1917 had been, if not great writers, as Octavio Paz used to assert, then certainly great institution-builders. Thanks to them, we now have universities such as the Colegio de México, publishing houses like the Fondo de Cultura Económica, the Bank of Mexico, and the National Institute of Anthropology and History (Instituto Nacional de Antropología e Historia), among others.

However, by the time the generation of 1968 came of age, there was no room to build new institutions. Then the dilemmas would be different. Like no other intellectual generation in the country's recent history, the generation of 1968 would have to face a veritable Leviathan in the form of the centralized and bureaucratic government which had emerged from a social revolution. Given the existence of this Philanthropic Ogre, intellectuals would have to choose their position. There would be two options, or at least so it would seem to them—to be on the inside or the outside.[30] "We were born," Krauze claims, "to public life with a well-defined calling: to attempt to change the state of affairs that had led the system to commit those crimes."[31] Intellectuals would no longer shape the state as in the past; the state would make them. From being the builders of the modern political system, intellectuals became its creations. One part of the generation of young people was devoured by the bureaucratic whale; the other part fashioned itself in opposition to it. According to Krauze:

> The political paths followed by the Generation have been very diverse, but the general tone has been the dissidence of the left-wing, expressed or exercised in academic, journalistic, political party, and in some cases, revolutionary circles. . . .Except for, in several cases, their personal work in literature, history, or the arts, members of the intellectual generation of 1968 succeeded in overcoming the isolationism of Mexican culture once and for all, and broke the "Cactus Curtain." . . .they introduced academic Marxism to Mexico. They published texts of social criticism and reports against the government and the capitalist order in the *Revista de la Universidad* and in *Siempre!'s* cultural supplement, "Mexico en la Cultura."[32]

The introduction of academic Marxism narrowed the intellectual horizons of the era rather than broadening them. By the seventies, its theories had acquired hegemony in the interpretation of social reality in Mexico. Marxism, adapted to the Mexican environment, displayed an "unadulterated economic determinism and postulated authoritarian and exclusive politics, the most radical version of which made it incapable of holding a dialogue with other worldviews."[33] As Ricardo Pozas contends, "the pronounced ideological content of informing the practice of social science research was linked to a growing militancy in university centers, and tended to impoverish theoretical practice and reflection."[34] The divine trinity, Louis Althusser, Martha Harnecker, and Nicos Poulantzas, would render critical reflection unnecessary. The "Cactus Curtain" had not been torn; academic Marxism was nothing but an ideological cloak worn by Mexican intellectuals in their indulgent country. The certainties that Marxism provided would make it unnecessary to perceive other realities. As a result, the adoption of the Marxist creed was an act of faith, but provided nothing in the way of opening, no matter how cosmopolitan its jargon may sound inside the university.

Furthermore, the most prominent members of the generation of 1968 have not devoted themselves entirely to academic life; save a few exceptions, they are not teachers. Nor have they founded parties capable of remaining in the public arena. It is true that the Popular Action Movement (MAP) participated in the foundation of the Unified Socialist Party of Mexico (PSUM). However, by the time the factions of the Mexican left finally united to form the Democratic Revolution Party (PRD), the content represented by the MAP ideals and participation of its members had already been almost completely diluted. It is unquestionably extremely ironic that currently the principal alternative in power should be the National Action Party (PAN).[35] Neither the intellectuals nor the spirit of the generation of 1968 had anything to do with the building of this party. There is, on the other hand, no *modern* left-wing option visible.

In other realms of culture, of the two most recent and important intellectual magazines, *Nexos* and *Vuelta* (1976-1998), only the first was founded by members of the generation of 1968. The second represented yet another example of Octavio Paz's intellectual vigor. Only after the death of Paz in 1998 did Enrique Krauze launch a project of his own, the journal *Letras Libres*, intended to be the successor of *Vuelta*. No other cultural supplement has succeeded in serving as such a catalyst for the cultural life of the country the way *La Cultura en México* has.[36] Among the other writings of 1968s intellectuals, there also is no equivalent of, for example, *Historia moderna de México*, Daniel Cosío Villegas' masterpiece. Cosío Villegas was the founder of El Colegio de México, and a major public intellectual from the 1940s to the 1970s. The wide-ranging scholarship of Cosío Villegas is clearly missing in today's intellectual scene. The books of the generation, with a handful of exceptions, are marked by the immediate. Nor has any important cultural or educational institution been founded in the last thirty years. If anything, those already in existence have languished. Time has taken its toll: as the young people matured, as with the children of the American counterculture of the 1960s, something faded in their discourse on a rupture with the past. The culture of 1968 ended up devoting itself to martyrdom, and revering the memory of what might have been and never was. It is not, however, its mythic calendar that draws attention, but rather the distance separating the country that exists today from that of its ideals. At the end of the century, ideological options for change are noticeably lacking. No modern social-democratic alternative has succeeded in taking shape; the *intelligentsia* of 1968 were sequestered by the orthodoxy: the revolutionary orthodoxy (the guerrillas of the seventies) and the national populist (the PRI). The intellectuals of that generation were unable to articulate new and modern descriptions of what the country could be. The timid efforts of some of its members failed with neither pain nor glory. The intellectuals of 1968 would not be the avant-garde of the revolution, but rather a nostalgic rear guard, their motto: "October 2 will not be forgotten." In the process, we have all lost.

It would be unjust and somewhat absurd to blame all of this on the Mexican intellectuals of the generation of 1968. Perhaps what has happened is that the intellectual frontier, that land of colonization, adventure, and challenge, has become a ghost town. It could be that the era of the explorers has simply come to an end. And yet, the consolidation of the modern Mexican state presents a paradox. We have become modern while enjoying few of the advantages of modernity. One would think that the efforts made over the last forty years to impart literacy and education would have created a wider intellectual market in Mexico; this has not been the case. The country has acquired many of the distinctive trappings of mass society, but the critical thinkers who constitute a following for the intellectual has never really appeared.[37] Thus, while television has become the means of communication that reaches millions, the number of readers simply has not grown at the same rate as the population. Because, in relative terms, Mexicans read less and less, the public sphere has become smaller. The absence of a wider following and market has significantly deformed the nature of intellectual work in Mexico. It has forced publications to depend on the government or on large corporations to survive. Something similar has occurred in the United States. There, the market does indeed exist, but it actually constricts the options and the arenas. The number of newspapers in that country has declined significantly over the last three decades. There are ever fewer spaces for expression, and the general tendency is toward uniformity. The market has also imposed its tastes and the demand for an "easy read" has significantly limited the room American publishers have to work with. These publishers must, at all costs, satisfy readers whose willingness to think is diminishing continually: a fast read is simply the complement to fast food. As is the case where many other things are concerned, the Mexican intellectual world seems to be the mirror image of the American one.

In addition to the expansion of the university system, the consolidation of the government, and the reduction of an already diminished public sphere, there is another factor that bears mentioning. The intellectual vitality in Mexico between 1935 and 1960 was, among other things, a result of the inflow of exiled Spanish republicans. In the late thirties, Mexico opened its doors to republican intellectuals fleeing the Spanish Civil War. Franco's victory turned the visit of men like Gaos and Pedroso into a permanent one.[38] The exiles enormously enriched Mexican culture. The House of Spain (*Casa de España*) in Mexico (which later became El Colegio de Mexico) and the National Autonomous University trained such Mexican intellectuals as Samuel Ramos, Luis Villoro, Emilio Uranga, and Leopoldo Zea in European philosophy. José Gaos, a Spanish student of Ortega y Gasset, translated *Being and Time* by Martin Heidegger.[39] However, like everything else, the intellectual vitality contributed by the Spanish exiles dissipated with time. The experience was not to be repeated.

The impoverishment of intellectuals in the United States is similar. It is an enormous irony that the American university system, with its hundreds of thousands of professors and millions of students, is incapable of producing public intellectuals. The domestic production crisis is such that in recent years the United States has had to resort to importing intellectuals from other parts of the world to fill the vacancies. This process began, and was most evident, among the left. As older intellectuals disappeared from the scene, they had to be replaced. For more than a decade, the influential *New York Review of Books* has regularly employed English intellectuals, professors from Oxford and Cambridge, for its reviews. Unlike the majority of their American colleagues, the English still know how to write with style and elegance. The English colonization of publications began at the same time as the disappearance of the new and younger voices from their pages. The *New York Review*'s lack of interest in cultivating new talent is legendary. According to Jacoby, for more than twenty five years the publication has been making withdrawals from the cultural bank without making any deposits. In consequence, "today, the operation must rely on imported intellectual capital, mainly from England."[40] This process can be seen in many other places. For example, on the editorial staff of *The New Republic*, the right-hand man of the editor-in-chief, Martin Peretz, is Andrew Sullivan, a young English conservative. Apparently, today Americans are even incapable of formulating their own nationalistic and xenophobic allegations. The author of a recent book against immigration, *Alien Nation*, is Peter Brimelow, another naturalized Brit.[41]

For years, native talent nourished conservatism; its tradition favored lucid prose over academic jargon.[42] But even there, professionalization has inflicted damage, and the provisions of fresh talent are no longer forthcoming. The number of young people in the conservative ranks has diminished considerably in recent years. American intellectual conservatism may well be dead. For several decades, says Michael Lind, the foundations of conservatism, which were located predominantly in the south and west of the United States, had as its evangelist Catholic and Jewish intellectuals educated in East Coast universities.[43] The tension between the conservative social base and the intellectual elite was always present, but, Lind says, it became unbearable when, in the past decade, to the ranks of American conservatism arrived a contingent of British analysts and journalists, a sort of Thatcherian Diaspora. The British colonists rapidly filled positions of importance in magazines, newspapers, and foundations. Stuart Butler became head of the Heritage Foundation and John O'Sullivan editor of the *National Review*. A Belgian immigrant, Arnaud de Borchgrave, installed himself in the editorial room of *The Washington Times*. If Jewish and Catholic intellectuals were foreign to the vast majority of traditionalists in the United States, the British alienated it completely. The result was that the door was opened up for a religious and anti-intellectual, but homegrown, religious right to serve as a catalyst for the discontent of the conservative following. Reverend Pat Robertson, of the Christian Coalition, speaks the language of the majority of conservatives "more authentically than Bill Buckley or Irving Kristol (to say nothing of Her Majesty's loyal subject John O'Sullivan)."[44] Most conservative intellectuals have taken on the role of mere intermediaries, if not image consultants, of the new conservative leaders.

Any intellectual movement that hopes to last, Lind points out, should maintain a continuous supply of new recruits, selecting the finest young talents from the outside and separating out the mediocre ones from the inside. American conservatism, on the other hand, has become a dynastic movement, where the sons, nephews, and stepchildren of the high priests inherit the places and honors of their elders in magazines and institutions. It is no accident that one of the few young conservative intellectuals that stands out currently, Dinesh D'Souza, is a young immigrant from India. The decline of merit has lowered the intellectual level of the main conservative publications. Magazines that considered themselves serious, like the *National Review, Commentary,* and *First Things,* now publish articles attacking Darwin's theory of evolution and pitiable allegations on the supposed genetic inferiority of racial minorities. By the mid-eighties, the American conservative movement, which was in the hands of a handful of elderly men, was completely at sea: it was being dragged along by the undertow of complacency and eccentricity. It was in desperate need of an internal renovation as well as the injection of new blood and new talent. However, this renewal and the necessary critical examination could not come about due to the structural dependency of conservative magazines and publications on foundation money. One by one, Lind asserts, all important publications or "think tanks" ended up becoming critically dependent upon the financial support of a handful of foundations. This has significantly shaped their editorial judgment and content. The fear of losing their backing has made editors cautious and has promoted self-censure. Pleasing their bosses, not their readers, has become the main preoccupation of conservative American magazines. The absence of a readership capable of rendering intellectual work even moderately self-sustainable has initiated a cycle of decadence. It is not very different from what is happening to the rest of the American intellectual scene. A Mexican can perceive a certain sense of irony in the intellectual colonization Americans have suffered at the hands of the English in recent years. However, on the other side of the border, there is not much cause for boasting, either.

The Sequestered Intelligentsia

The impoverishment of public culture and debate in the last thirty years has not been entirely obvious. Fanfare has often distracted attention from the signs of decadence. For example, Carlos Monsiváis, a prominent leftist intellectual and an icon of the 1968 generation, posed this question in 1975:

> How can anyone speak of disaster in the midst of this fervor of publishing houses, growth of the reading public, packed lectures, recitals, film clubs and libraries, concerts, scholarships, prizes, galleries, journals, cultural supplements in newspapers, serious and promising endeavors in smaller cities, literary workshops, demographic explosion in the university, daily cocktail parties for poets and novelists, miniature art museums available at every corner news stand, the vinyl revolution, the multiplication of theater groups, the growing number of classical dance enthusiasts?[45]

Some of the indicators of this intellectual bonanza were misleading. The indiscriminate demographic explosion in universities produced the bureaucracy and gigantism that Bartra would deplore twenty years later. Rather than indicating a sustained cultural expansion, what the seventies presented was a colorful display of fireworks. The splendor was momentary and superficial. In the following years, the number of readers would not increase; on the contrary, in relative terms it decreased. In Mexico there would be fewer, not more, bookstores and the recurrent economic crises would make books a luxury item. A survey carried taken in 1995 for the Mexican Foundation for the Promotion of Reading (*Fundación Mexicana para el Fomento de la Lectura*) revealed that almost 67 percent of respondents read between 1 and 15 books a year. Almost 30 percent read fewer than 6 books.[46] In fact, and in spite of the contradictory signals, the public sphere was shrinking. In the eighties and nineties, Mexican publishers would suffer the same symptoms: economic crisis, scarcity of readers, and a deficient distribution. As expressed in one analysis, "In Mexico, the cultural publishing market for books is restricted, and what is most troubling is that it contracts further every year."[47] According to the 1990 population census, Mexico had nearly 82 million inhabitants, with only 25 million of these likely to be possible readers. The estimated number of readers is 1.5 million; the average demand for books consumption among the population is barely half a book per person per year. Television is not the only factor affecting the number of readers, but also, neither the school nor the family fosters the habit of reading. The few books Mexicans buy will typically be only half-read. According to the National Chamber of the Book Industry, (*Cámara Nacional de la Industria del Libro*), only 2 out of every 100 books bought will be read completely, 6 will be read half-way through, 65 will be read to little past the fiftieth page, and 27 will only be leafed through, or given as a gift.[48] The decline in the reading public is a binational phenomenon, although the proportion is obviously different. In the United States, the number of books published is decreasing. For example, in 1993, 49,757 titles, including both new books and subsequent editions, were published. However, by 1994, that figure had fallen to 40,584.[49]

The fact that no one reads in Mexico comes as no surprise to anyone; it is common knowledge. The absence of readers is lamented as one of those inevitable phenomena of nature beyond our control. Occasionally, however, someone reflects upon the consequences that an ever smaller following will have on intellectual work. Among other things, the contraction of readership has made it possible to engage in a monologue. Friends, who have always been important, have in many cases become more important than the ideas themselves. One's career, and any opportunity to stand out in the intellectual milieu, frequently hinges not upon merit as established by a following, but upon informal relationships between a handful of people who determine destinies in the Republic of Letters. There, the public cheers for no one. The growing personalization has turned intellectual debates into personal conflicts, where the temptation to indulge in a diatribe is rarely resisted. Since an intellectual's future depends on his long-standing membership to a determined group, loyalty takes on an enormous importance. The consequence of this particular type of organization of the *literati* is that internal dissent is not tolerated, and the ranks close in when faced with any outside criticism. Thus, it has become impossible to debate in nonpersonal terms. The very possibility of holding public discussion is debatable.

From the description that Monsiváis gives of the cultural paraphernalia of the seventies, we can deduce the importance of social events in the intellectual world of Mexico. There is something paradoxical holding the life of the mind to be merely a series of social events. Although the number of books published in Mexico is decreasing, and although most of the time not more than a few thousand copies are published at once, not a day passes without a book being presented with a grand party to celebrate. Thus, we observe a peculiar phenomenon, which is that in Mexico books are introduced to society, but not read.

In both countries, public debate has deteriorated. It would be difficult to exaggerate the consequences that feeble public sphere has had on the Mexican intellectual world. The health of a society critically depends upon the existence of vigorous public debate. Only when we submit our ideas to the test of debate, Lasch contends, can we understand what we know and what we still need to learn. Until we defend our ideas in public, they are but half-formed convictions. It is precisely the act of articulating and defending our ideas that gives them shape and definition. Then, perhaps others will recognize their own experiences in what we say. Debates are not won when we silence our opponent but rather when we manage to persuade him or her. And this occurs only when we can listen calmly to opposing arguments, and convince the opponent that nonetheless there is a flaw in his or her line of reasoning. In the course of this process we may well discover that our own arguments are not as solid as we once believed.[50]

In the United States, in spite of the enormous quantity of information transmitted by mass media, the average citizen knows less about public affairs than before. Paradoxically this is partly a result of the modernization of the printed press. American newspapers of the current century are markedly different from those in circulation a hundred years ago. Newspapers then presented more than just information, they presented opinions. In them, readers expected to find a definitive point of view on public affairs, as well as merciless criticism of contrary positions. It is impossible to ignore the obvious similarity between nineteenth-century American dailies and many current Mexican newspapers. Mexicans often deplore this type of press which offers a wealth of opinion, but a dearth of information. However, in the United States, the flourishing of this kind of journalism, between 1830 and 1900, was simultaneous with the period of the "greatest political participation in the history of the United States."[51] At that time, 80 percent of those eligible to vote actually went to the polls on election days.[52] Newspapers were a printed extension of the popular assemblies; not only did they inform their readers about political controversies, they actively participated in them. In the following century the concept of what the press should be changed radically: from then on, its main function would be to provide its readers with objective information. No longer would there be a place for opinion and debate in newspapers. Government politics would no longer be an art, but a science, by definition, a matter for the experts. In this conception of politics, which would become dominant in the United States, public debate would be seen, at best, as a necessary evil. If sufficient scientific information existed in all matters, controversy would become completely unnecessary. Since the press would present information objectively, there would no longer be any controversy because, according to Walter Lippman, things would appear in their true dimension. Debate would occur only where there was insufficient information. However, the search for reliable information is guided by precisely the same questions that arise in the course of debate and disagreement over a given policy. When presented void of context, facts alone have no meaning. The effect of this scientific vision of public information can be seen every day on American television. There, the viewer passively observes a profusion of so-called "news." Fiscal deficit indicators happily share airtime with the latest scandals of the most popular singer and diets for obesity. It is an absolute variety show of frivolity.

In Mexico, on the other hand, it would appear that we are at the opposite extreme. In a way, we could say, with no irony, that Mexicans enjoy some of the advantages of premodernity. They also suffer its disadvantages. Not having experienced the "objectivity" revolution, Mexican newspapers favor editorials over information. It is the declarations of government officials and the opinions of intellectuals regarding public events that are considered news. The importance given to intellectuals' opinions would be excessive, were it not for the fact that Mexican newspapers print only a few of the tens of thousands of copies they receive, and are read in only a few cities throughout the country. The vast majority of Mexicans do not care what newspapers say. Thus, a curious reenactment takes place, where intellectuals have the starring role in a drama that no one watches. The drama repeats itself time and again. In both countries, however, democracy depends upon the existence of a vigorous public debate. Something which is lacking on either side of the border.

In an essay published in 1960, at the time of a shift in Mexican culture, Luis Villoro, a prominent philosopher and intellectual, asserted:

The importance of these last fifty years of culture lies not so much in the quantity or quality of the works produced, as in a spiritual movement that runs through all of them. The last half-century has been a decisive for our spirit: it will, without a doubt, go down as a period in which the community attempted to discover its true being and free itself from its illusions.[53] The world to the *Ateneo de la Juventud*[54] was marked by hurriedness. There is no time to meditate in retreat. Everything invites extroversion. There is an urgency to write, to narrate. The intellectual's own world enters through his senses within him and at the same time outside of him; he begins feverishly to reflect, his language fixes upon the first discovery. Vasconcelos' philosophy does not allow for retreat, there is no room in it for inner silence; it obliges one to open himself to the exterior and completely merge with the cosmos.

After that point, Mexican culture would reflect a growing sense of introspection. The fact that intellectuals were retreating from the outside world could be intuited in the search for the features of Mexican tradition, in its mentality, in its characteristic psychology. With the passing of the years and the generations, Villoro claims, "the self-absorption is accompanied also by withdrawal. Culture becomes more subjective and polished, saturated with a soft skepticism and a certain inner distance." The disruptive note in this process has perhaps been the cosmopolitanism of some intellectuals. Jorge Cuesta, a member of the *Contemporáneos* generation, would say that Mexicans had deliberately chosen a universal culture. It was a search for originality; this was not thought to be found in a collection of inherited goods, but rather in the free selection from culture in its universal forms.[55] However, every cosmopolitan episode is a discordant note in an increasingly uniform concert. Cultural nationalism, much more overpowering, would become firmly established in the foundations of Mexican culture. The celebration of the endemic would not, as cosmopolitans hoped, bear out the theory that, "that which distinguishes us from the rest of the world will have to open us up to the universal." In 1960, Villoro noted the decline of the Mexican cultural movement. A certain nonsuccess then became evident: the destruction of previous conceptions, such as that of Porfirian positivism, had not been followed by the creation of new visions. In the past, positivism, before it faded away, offered a rational system capable of permitting an "understanding of the world as a whole, of giving meaning to action, and of firmly guiding collective education." All of these advantages had been lost with the defeat of the intellectual orthodoxy. At the same time, Villoro foresaw a difficult road ahead. To face the crisis of all that was lacking he said, "will be no easy task, nor one of a single generation. All in all, what we are dealing with is a new urgent mission. To fulfill it, we will need to indoctrinate our culture in the universal currents of thought."[56]

Four decades later, it is possible to say that the crisis of that time has not been resolved, that the answers have not appeared and that, on the contrary, we are languishing in uncertainty. Nor has our culture merged with universal currents of thought. Thus, we have wasted the Mexican Revolution's most precious legacy to the intelligentsia: "Making the appropriation of universal culture possible, without losing authenticity." Villoro, looking back, recognized the undeniable importance of the fifty years that transpired between 1910 and 1960. Could the same be said in regards to the last forty years that have elapsed?

Today, a singular type of asphyxiation plagues us. Perhaps seventy years ago the intellectual health of the country did not require a vigorous public sphere. Imagination was flourishing in the premodern spaces of "sociability" described by François-Xavier Guerra.[57] However, modern culture requires more stimulation. A mass society requires newspapers to arrive, and to be read by millions of people. It requires a great number of forums for pluralistic discussions: magazines, supplements, and universities. In Mexico, at the beginning of the new century, we have none of this. On the other hand, there is a reverence rarely seen in history for figures from the past. Today, to a great extent, we are living in their shadow. This reverence, which at times borders upon devotion, denotes not only respect, but also a sense of unease about venturing out onto new paths without the blessing of our elders. Ambition has also dwindled: from the carefully considered and extensive reflections upon philosophy which used to occupy intellectuals, we have fallen into the recurrent practice where writers no longer write books, but rather publish collections of their journalistic articles. No one seems to mind this form of recycling intellectual work.

From Vicarious Conflicts to Personal Attacks

The questions that inevitably arise upon taking a bird's-eye view of the last forty years in Mexican intellectual debate are: What happened to the discussions about the soul of the culture that, in the past, captured the imagination of Mexican intellectuals? To the debates over the spiritual infrastructure of the nation, over the philosophic relativism expressed in the role of books and of education, which were at the center of the controversy over Dewey, both in Mexico and in the United States? Where are the impassioned debates between nationalists and cosmopolitans? The controversies of the seventies, eighties and nineties demonstrate the impoverishment of public debate. In Mexico and the United States, the common characteristic of this process is a kind of derailment. From that time on, debates would have less and less to do with the real problems in both societies. The public arena has been taken up by what we could call vicarious conflicts, other people's quarrels, in which intellectuals participate as accessories.

In Mexico, after 1968, there was perhaps a consensus on only one point: the political system was broken.[58] From then on, this point would become a tirelessly repeated cliche. However, as the experience of the following decade would bear out, the political system, however depleted it may appear, was *not* broken. So far from it, in fact, that it would survive mutating for nearly thirty more years. The death certificate was expedited prematurely. What is certain is that very little was known about the subtle and complex structures of the postrevolutionary political system in its national, regional, and local levels. Serious investigation was noticeably absent in the decades following 1968. One would have hoped that 1968 would have produced far-reaching works of political and sociological analysis on what had happened to the country. Such was not the case. Apart from fragmented studies on the political reality of Mexico, the most important work from the period, *La democracia en Mexico* (*Democracy in Mexico*), was written in 1965, before the student movement and by someone who was not even a member of that generation, Pablo González Casanova.[59] The *zeitgeist* would spare no one: none of the later works by González Casanova would have the same reach as did *La democracia en México*. His work, on the contrary, became more petty, along with the spirit of the following decades.

The surprise caused in Mexico by the events of 1994 (the return of the guerrilla warriors, political assassinations, and financial turbulence) was due, to a great extent, to the fact that many of the political and social processes of the preceding decades had passed unnoticed. In reality, many of the dynamics in the political system that was presumed to have collapsed twenty-six years earlier were not understood.[60] How could the dying system have survived for so many years? No one was offering satisfactory answers to this question.

If for years, intellectuals failed to correctly dissect the political system that had shown its ugliest face in Tlatelolco, what were they doing? The answer to this question lies in the history of vicarious conflicts in Mexico. Up against the breakdown of the political system, asserts Sanchez Susarrey, two crucial questions arose. The first concerned the alternative the country should follow: the third way, or socialism? The second question referred to the role of the intellectual in society: should he actively participate or should he remain on the sidelines, maintaining a critical distance from the regime and from popular movements? From a bit of distance, what stands out is not the validity of these positions, but rather the complete irrelevance of the entire issue. The polemic over the third way was, in the end, a debate over the merits of socialism and capitalism as philosophical political systems. At the same time, it must be said, all the world was engaged in this debate. Certainly, however, in some places it was more important than in others. In Cuba, the interest in the future of socialism was not at all academic, and the Americans, who were among the principal opponents in the ideological conflict, were obviously very interested in exposing the crimes of Soviet totalitarianism. This was the Cold War.

However, public discussion in Mexico on this issue had overlooked a fundamental fact: the debate over the two options was taking place in a context in which neither of the presumed alternatives could possibly be chosen. At that time, the obvious was not so evident. What was happening, and not only in Mexico, was that the Cold War had colonized public debate. Its themes, and its ideological passion, had been internalized by Mexican intellectuals, and they were now the focus of the controversy between intellectuals of the left and "liberal" intellectuals.[61] Looking back, what is surprising is that neither of these positions was linked to a solution involving real political change. Discounting the ideological passion, the dispute resembles one those indefatigable medieval discussions over the gender of angels. It is quite likely that the left argued its points badly, "with timidity, and without rigor or critical freedom," as Octavio Paz claimed, but what did that matter? None of the intellectuals of the left would become a member of the politburo, nor of the avant-garde of any revolution but the Mexican Revolution (the PRI).[62] The dimension and the reach of the guerrilla in the seventies only confirmed the obvious: in Mexico, socialist revolution had absolutely no chance of success. It went completely unnoticed that any existing Mexican "fellow travelers" were only a parody of the true ones in England and the United States. The response of the left was along the same lines. "Given a phenomenon as vast as socialism," replied Monsiváis, "what is urgently needed is systematic criticism, not wholesale negation." Self-complacency, the conviction that history was on their side, was a trait common to both sides of the debate. "The left," Monsiváis goes on to claim, "is generating the more critical, profound and original interpretations of the nation's reality and its linkage with the world."[63]

The adversaries were overlooking a fundamental fact: no Cold War was being waged in Mexico; there had never been a true socialist movement in the country, and liberalism was no more than a fiction invented during the second half of the nineteenth century. Like socialism, liberalism had never managed to become an actual governmental practice in Mexico, not even during the mythic Restored Republic of Juárez. The national revolutionary regime was a singular authoritarian mix of corporatism, nationalism, and mixed economy. The controversy was a metropolitan importation that fell short of the mark. The reality of the country during those years would not change one bit, no matter who won the debate on the merits of real socialism. However, the spell of the ideology was too powerful. Some saw Bolsheviks on every corner, wearing traditional Mexican *charro* suits, ready to erect gulags in the Yucatán, while others looked dreamily toward "a world impregnated with socialism."[64] The magnitude of the illusion can only be appreciated in retrospect.

Certainly there more than one element of injustice in this post-gain analysis, but it cannot be denied that intellectuals of that period were riding on a Great Diversion of monumental proportions. A reading of the inflamed articles of that period gives the impression that intellectuals were convinced that the future of the socialist alternative was being played out in Mexico. Or even, it was as if they were occupying the front lines in the Cold War, instead of a periphery capitalist country, irrelevant to the geostrategic dynamic of the conflict between the two superpowers.

This illusion did not disappear when the socialism that really existed did. After the Berlin Wall fell, some would attempt to extract a public act of contrition from intellectuals of the left, a collective *mea culpa*. As if the work of Mexican left-wing intellectuals had been crucial to the maintenance of the Soviet bureaucratic state. There was something truly ridiculous in all of this. Behind this unintended farce lies a singular impotence, a lack of the intellectual energy to perceive and confront the real problems.

A by-product of the Cold War was the strengthening of anti-American feeling in Mexico. As Monsiváis puts it:

anti-imperialism, a central element in popular thought and sentiment in Latin America, depends on categorical experiences (invasions, territorial take-overs, installation of dictators, systematized economic plundering), and on an unequivocal version of the American: the Other, the aggressor, the invader, the predator, the heretic even.[65] The United States would be held fully responsible for almost all of the evils of the countries in this hemisphere. American society (as a whole, profoundly racist and classist) sets the pattern for the new types of racism and classism in Latin America.[66]

Evidently, nothing good could come from the empire, much less good ideas. Monsiváis' position would become paradigmatic of the intellectual left. Thus, an American professor, Paul Hollander, after having traveled to Mexico to probe the aversion of Mexican intellectuals toward the United States, concluded that it was they (along with the intellectuals of the future, that is, the students), who were carrying the torch of anti-Americanism in Mexico. For Hollander, the United States was the scapegoat for Mexican intellectuals, allowing them to release their frustration over the condition of marginality that characterized their life. He also identified the structural dependence of intellectuals on the government as a factor that explained the nationalist fervor which many of them displayed.[67] The Cold War also gave rise to a pro-Americanism exemplified by the emergence of technocrats and other imitators of north-of-the border consumerism.

The last thirty-five years also saw a growing interest in the public role of the intellectual. In the past, Krauze says, the collaboration of intellectuals with those in power, "seemed to mark the proper culmination of their intellectual trajectory."[68] In the seventies, this perception began to change "to the point of reaching the opposite extreme: now all collaboration and even proximity of the intellectual to those in power not only seems dishonest but indecent." The relation between the intellectual and "the powers" has been the subject of a great amount of reflection all over the world.[69] An endless number of books have been written on the explicit or implicit commitments of intellectuals. Such words as "betrayal," "collaborationism," and "organic relationship" are terms that appear recurrently in the dialogue over intellectuals.[70]

The preoccupation with establishing clearly and precisely the lines of demarcation dividing the intellectual territory of Mexico coincided with the decrease of the real importance of intellectuals. For Vasconcelos, to speak of the autonomy of the work of an intellectual would have seemed absurd. Here is the paradox: it is when intellectuals are *no longer* politicians, or founders of political parties, or builders of institutions, that a preoccupation over their public role arises. Independence or commitment, critical distance or proximity. It is when their social roles are *less* tangible that their work seems to be more relevant. It is then that the actions of intellectuals are subject to a more intense public scrutiny. The upshot of this is that intellectuals stop being direct participants in politics and become a sort of superstars of ideas, who sometimes participate in politics and sometimes do not. Their actions, statements, journalistic articles, meetings, occasional aphorisms, and of course, their friendships, become a matter of public judgment and speculation. The public relations apparatus of intellectuals have become more and more like that of government officials. Tight agendas, private secretaries, power lunches, and a general inaccessibility appear to constitute the paraphernalia of Mexican intellectuals. Of course, this has deformed the perception intellectuals have of their own importance in society. The crowning of intellectuals as superstars has had a negative effect on their work. Bit by bit, the illusion that it is they, and not their ideas, that matter has become accepted in the public arena. Ergo, the conflicts between intellectuals have ever less to do with ideas and ever more to do with their personas. Thus, public debate has become personalized.

The process of decay has been progressive. The vicarious conflicts that occupied the attention of the intellectuals in the seventies have degenerated into personal attacks. Here ideas have been completely disappeared; the fall has been simply astonishing. From the debates on profound cultural issues that took place in the twenties, we have ended up with disputes over who occupies which bureaucratic position. There is no other way to read the latest round in the public ring. According to Sánchez Susarrey, the controversy generated by the various international meetings organized by the two most important groups of intellectuals in the last ten years, "should not be understood as the sum of individual or group quarrels."[71] This assertion is difficult to defend. The personal confrontations were disguised as clashes over public morality. Susarrey contended that:

It was inadmissible for one camp to benefit from public institutions. The government was under the obligation not to take sides; it was unfair for it to wear the badge of a single group. The problem was one of social hygiene and public morality: without an impartial state, modernity would be impossible in the field of politics and religion, not to mention the cultural arena.

Along the same lines ran Octavio Paz's charges that one group intended to "take control over the principal centers of cultural life in Mexico."[72] An outsider might think what was at stake were the institutions of a vibrant cultural world, not crumbs being bickered over, which is in fact what was taking place. As if the "centers of cultural life" in Mexico were more than just a handful of stagnant organizations, whose influence affected only an infinitesimal fraction of Mexicans. How have we come to this regrettable state? This question cannot be answered perhaps without considering the contraction of the public sphere over the last four decades. Mexico has become a mass society, but its cultural life has not expanded in kind. The degradation of public debate is only one of the effects of this process. The country is becoming ever larger, its cultural life ever smaller. Something similar is taking place in the United States, where, according to Lasch, a singular phenomenon has occurred: the elites have rebelled. They have disengaged themselves from their historical responsibilities toward the rest of society. Selfishness and apathy are the identifying traits of the new American elite.[73] For the ordinary American citizen, the problems the country is facing are clear enough: urban violence, a drop in the standard of living of all but a few, the disaster in public education. One would think that these issues would be at the center of debates on the future of American society. This is not the case. On the contrary, the most heated debates have been waged over what is taught in a dozen elite universities. The campus battles in the United States are also vicarious conflicts. Culture wars, Jacoby claims, distract public attention from what is happening in most American universities. Only 3 percent of university students attend expensive private colleges.[74]

A debate is taking place over whether the works of Dead White Men should be studied, or on the contrary, the creations of women and of Mayans, while in most institutions of higher learning in the United States (the ones that do not make news), students are surviving under economically precarious conditions. A college education means learning technical and practical subjects, such as accounting. There is an energetic debate on college campuses over whether certain words that hurt the sensibilities and self-esteem of some students should be used. Since the social phenomenon described by a given word (such as racism or sexism), cannot be changed, the solution has been to eliminate the use of the term.[75] The campaign of semantic purification has revealed the impossibility of acting on reality itself. Similarly, in Mexico, social criticism over the last thirty years has often taken refuge in verbal acrobatics that contain more clever witticisms than profound ideas. Lasch notes:

> In their drive to insulate themselves against risk and contingency, against the unpredictable hazards that afflict human life, the thinking classes have seceded not just from the common world around them but from reality itself. The culture wars that have convulsed America since the sixties are best understood as a form of class warfare, in which an enlightened elite (as it thinks of itself) seeks not so much to impose its values on the majority (a majority perceived as incorrigibly racist, sexist, provincial, and xenophobic), much less to persuade the majority by means of rational public debate, as to create parallel or "alternative" institutions in which it will no longer be necessary to confront the unenlightened at all.[76]

Not only do the culture wars distract attention from more serious and pressing problems, but also a large part of the specialized knowledge in social sciences generated in United States' universities is totally irrelevant for society as a whole. For instance, articles published in academic political science journals are no longer read by decision makers, who typically find them not only unintelligible, but also completely useless for solving real problems.[77] The state of American universities is provoking a feeling of general malaise.[78] The insularity of universities, which offers protection from the outside world, has also seriously deformed intellectual work. Overspecialization has now made it practically impossible for academics in different fields to carry on a dialogue. Extreme individualism, and a lack of collegiality, mark the academic profession in the United States. No one who has not obtained a doctorate has access to the academic market. Earning a doctorate, however, takes five to ten years of study and research. Entry-level salaries, for those who are lucky enough to find a job as a professor in a shrinking market, are remarkably low. The result is that the best students avoid the academic majors carrying no social prestige. The schools of law, medicine, and business recruit the best students among the most ambitious. The mediocre students, the socially inept, remain in universities never again to emerge. This is, perhaps, a sociological explanation for the fact that American intellectuals do not enjoy social prestige in their country. This is a problem. "One does not need to assert," Richard Hofstadter contends, "that intellectuals should get sweeping indulgence or exercise great power, in order to insist that respect for intellect and its functions is important to the culture and the health of any society, and that in ours this respect has often been notably lacking."[79]

The ailments of American intellectuals are the exact opposite of those that plague Mexicans. The two pathologies are the mirror image of each other. On one side there is an excessive preeminence deforming the role of the intellectual, on the other we find an insecure and diminished character, with no public role to play. In Mexico, cultivated thinkers enjoy a peculiar legitimacy that confers on them a privileged place in society. Of course, not everyone is rejoicing over the enthroning of intellectuals as public figures. Gabriel Zaid has criticized this process in his essay "De los libros al poder" ("From Books to Power"), which, to be placed in context, should be read after Hofstadter's book on anti-intellectualism in the United States.[80]

Perhaps the appropriate solution would be to follow the wisdom of Aristotle and fight for a golden mean: neither a superstar nor a nobody. Mexican and American intellectuals could learn quite a bit from the strengths and weaknesses of their counterparts on both sides of the border. If we Mexicans become more rigorous, humble, and professional, emulating our colleagues across the Rio Bravo, we will be better off. On the other hand, if American intellectuals were to come out from their universities and take up the forgotten tradition of active intervention in public affairs, they would more closely resemble their counterparts south of the Rio Grande. Both of our countries would benefit from this change.

The Tragedy of Education

In the last thirty years, education levels in Mexico and the United States have tended to converge. This phenomenon denotes a pronounced drop in the quality of education in the United States. Between 1991 and 1994, a group of Mexican researchers conducted a comparative study of children in seven North American cities: Mexico City, Guadalajara, Monterrey, San Francisco, Philadelphia, Vancouver, and Montreal.[81] They tested students' knowledge in elementary and secondary schools in Mexico, the United States, and Canada to obtain information on the current state of education. The findings were significant. The city with the lowest average of the 7 was Philadelphia (38.2), followed by Guadalajara (40.6), Monterrey (42.5), Mexico City (45.3), Montreal (50.3), San Francisco (50.9), and Vancouver (59.3). The overall averages for primary schools were 42.9 in Mexico, 45.4 in the United States and 54.6 in Canada. In other words, the difference between the United States, and its southern neighbor was only 2.5 percent. These results are a sign of the virtual collapse of public education in the United States. Standardization has been to the lowest common denominator, with Americans falling back to third world educational levels. The alarm signals have been ringing without interruption for years. In the study, *What do our 17 year olds know?*, Dianne Ravitch and Chester Finn discovered that the majority of American teenagers were "culturally illiterate." Their knowledge of history and of many other subjects was just short of nil. Even more basic indicators show results that are scandalous for any industrialized country. In mathematics, grammar, and reading, the levels are generally low, and in the poorest regions of the country, teenagers graduate from high school not knowing how to read.

The public education system used to be the pride of American society; it served as a compensatory mechanism that evened out the distribution of opportunities. Americans were not prepared for education to become one of its most urgent social problems at the beginning of the new century. In contrast, Mexicans have historically seen education as the cornerstone of development. Like other underdeveloped countries, Mexico once placed in education its fondest hopes for progress. However, none of its educational efforts have had positive results. An unplanned growth in the number of schoolchildren in the last thirty years has lowered the "social effectiveness" of the educational system in Mexico.[82] In reality, and as the decreasing budgets allotted to education demonstrate, the Mexican government has tragically abandoned public education to its fate, thereby neglecting one of its basic responsibilities. The contrast with the twenties, when Vasconcelos undertook his educational crusade, is extremely telling: it is another sign of how the moral character of the Mexican intellectual elite has mutated. By the eighties, the incipient leveling effect of public education, which had been one of the achievements of the postrevolutionary governments, had completely withered away. A dual system took hold in Mexico: the elites are educated in private institutions from the most basic levels right up to college, while the majority of Mexicans receive a deficient education in public schools. The drastic difference between public and private education that exists in Mexico is starting to be seen in the United States, with all the entailing social consequences.

In Mexico, illiteracy has never been totally eradicated, and final proficiency after both elementary and middle school is low. Academic levels are deplorable. A test given to primary school children in the state of Aguascalientes in 1983 revealed the following results: 86.1 percent of them failed in math, 65.7 percent in Spanish, and 63.6 percent in natural sciences. In high school, things were not any better. On the entrance exam given by the National Autonomous University of Mexico for admission to preparatory school during the ten years between 1976 and 1985, the cut-off grade was, on average, 3.5 on a scale from 1 to 10. During the same period, the National University admitted students to the bachelor's program who had obtained an average of 4.5 on the entrance examination.[83] Higher education in Mexico is in a grievous state because of bureaucracy, lack of funds, and student political activism determined to obstruct all efforts toward reform. The 1999 student movement, which closed the university for almost a year, was the latest of these developments. Students in 1999 emulated their forerunners of 1968, but their movement was but a caricature of the latter. While students killed in the Tlatelolco massacre demanded democracy for all, their so-called successors asked for several exemptions and privileges for themselves. The government finally took over the facilities of the university and charged hundred of students of diverse felonies. The movement evidenced that the university lay in ruins. Once upon a time in Mexico the public university was, like basic education in the United States, a source of pride. Today all that remains is the recollection of those times.

What is the relation between the simultaneous fall in educational levels in the two countries and the deterioration of the public role of intellectuals? In a certain way, this phenomenon is a sign of a singular failure to uphold one's duty. Historically, as occurred in the twenties, intellectuals were concerned with building the spiritual infrastructure of their societies. The questions were generic: what type of citizens and what type of political communities are desirable? Distributive issues loomed large. Social justice was not a jingle but a cause. Thus the concern for education. Today, there is a void. Intellectuals in both countries have stopped caring about the education that the majority of the members of their societies receive. This, in turn, has broken the link through which ran a certain food for the soul, one that nourished intellectuals. Their indifference toward society has been reciprocated. The fewer the number of intellectually enlightened citizens that exist, the less intellectual work will be appreciated.

In both countries, the debate over education has been centered on universities. This is significant. At the beginning of the last century, intellectual involvement had a more general character. Dewey was concerned with the kind of education that all children, from the earliest grades, received. Rural education, promoted by Sáenz, sought to reconstruct the foundations of the country, from the ground up. For intellectuals in the early decades of the twentieth century, it was clear that the priority should be the formation of social capital, not only of the elites.

Universities have become the center of intellectual attention in the United States. In Mexico, the conflicts the National Autonomous University is experiencing are also of concern to intellectuals. This emphasis has significantly distorted public debate. No public university can enjoy complete health without a vigorous system of public basic, middle and upper middle education to support it.

Perhaps a measure of the distance that separates us from bygone times is Allan Bloom's book, *The Closing of the American Mind*. Bloom taught at the University of Chicago until his death in 1992.[84] This book, published in 1987, surprisingly became a best-seller. Bloom sharply criticized students in "the best universities in the United States." The vision of the world that they acquired in college tended to impoverish rather than enrich them intellectually. Bloom placed the blame for this process on relativism, which had been introduced surreptitiously into the American intellectual world. Bloom asserted:

Liberalism without natural rights, the kind we knew from John Stuart Mill and John Dewey, taught us that the only danger confronting us is being closed to the emergent, the new, and the manifestations of progress. No attention had to be paid to the fundamental principles or the moral virtues that inclined men to live according to them.[85]

For Bloom, Dewey, who believed that notions such as "soul" or "immutable truth" belonged to the infancy of philosophy, was himself a "big baby."[86] It did not take long for Bloom's critics, nor for his apologists, to come forth. Richard Rorty, for example, called the author of *The Closing of the American Mind* an authoritarian, and resuscitated Dewey to oppose the return to the classics that Bloom advised. "The defects of our high schools," Rorty asserts, "[can be] . . . made up for by a couple of years' worth of Great Books."[87] Harvey Mansfield, who sympathized with Bloom's ideas, replied that Rorty would hardly be able to remedy the grave deficiencies of high school students with just a few years of reading the classics. The culprit for education's predicament was, Mansfield claimed, Rorty's mentor: John Dewey.[88]

However, the most piercing criticism of Bloom was made by Russell Jacoby: *The Closing of the American Mind* was only concerned, as even its author recognized, with a handful of elite universities. The vast majority of college students in the United States, those who do not attend Harvard, Yale, Stanford, or Chicago, are not infected by odious relativism; they simply languish, forgotten. In one thing Dewey was clearly Bloom's superior: Dewey cared about more people.

Conclusion

The intellectual deterioration in the United States and Mexico occurred simultaneously with the collapse of the bridges between the intellectual communities of the two countries. The rapid process of extinction of public intellectuals in the United States and the progressive intellectual self-absorption on the part of Mexicans, explains this phenomenon to some extent. Public intellectuals, like John Dewey or Frank Tennenbaum, have virtually disappeared, and their place has been filled by the so-called experts in Mexican studies. They are specialists, not public intellectuals. They often know the country that is their object of study better than they know their own society. Their voice is rarely heard; like other specialists, they have not mastered a public prose. That is why one of them, Delal Baer, found it a nice surprise when, thanks to the debate over the North American Free Trade Agreement, the American government and other groups showed, for the first time, an interest in what the specialists had to say. As she put it: "As a result of the debate over NAFTA and Mexican democratization, being a Mexican specialist carries some weight in the halls of the United States Congress, in the media, in financial markets, in the political evolution of Mexico, and in bilateral relations."[89] This moment of fame, as is always the case, is ephemeral. In a short time, the professors will return to their cubicles, until the next Mexican crisis rescues them from oblivion and places them momentarily before the public eye once again.

Another co-occurrence was the simultaneous crisis of the intellectual generation of the seventies. Self-complacent rhetoric aside, it would seem, for different reasons, that on neither side of the border did the generation amount to much. Few generations have come to public life in a climate of such ideological and cultural effervescence as did that of the seventies. Few would promise, like it did, an intellectual blossoming of such magnitude. Few have been so disappointing.

The somewhat patricidal critical attitude that intellectuals hold toward their predecessors is, of course, nothing new. The very members of the generation of 1968 (who were born in the mid- to late forties and were between twenty and thirty years old in 1968), also felt it in their time. In 1972 Héctor Aguilar Camín and Enrique Krauze, noted the following in regard to the intellectual as a public figure:

> the character, obsessed by the overwhelming and immediate facade of national politics (an inescapable omnipresence of the Tlatoani on duty[90] among other things), runs along the edges of a subdued cultural life, and suddenly bumps into the urgent need for a political definition. The media, obsessed with the same and with the irresistible siren song of the news, also plays a part, acting, as if it had the answers. In fact, it responds to inquiries as if its words were the natural result of a trajectory that, besides, is under no one's scrutiny or restraint. In Mexico, where, if there was once a consistent project for national culture, it never grew into a living, lasting form that would today make up a recognizable legacy, problems are naturally more urgent. It seems that many of our intellectuals can only oppose this, which is our imprecise culture, with in the end a flight or a feint, not an oeuvre.[91]

The image of a fallen bridge is embodied by William Burroughs. The presence of the American writer in Mexico during the fifties was due, more than to intellectual concerns, to the urgency of circumstances: he arrived fleeing the justice system of his country. During the time Burroughs lived in Mexico:

> He never took an interest in modern Mexican culture, never said two words to any national luminary of the period, never attended any lectures or plays. Possibly, he never bought a book written by a Mexican. Forty years later he had never heard mention of Octavio Paz, Carlos Fuentes, or Juan Rulfo.[92]

Suspicion, not just admiration, is part of any turning of the generational guards. The motor that moves intelligence is the critical eye, not praise or deference. Looking outside is peering into hidden mirrors where we can observe ourselves from angles previously unknown. The images we see are always our own reflection, although we do not always recognize ourselves. However, only by looking will we know who we are.

Notes

1. Octavio Paz, *Postdata* (Mexico: Siglo XXI, 1970), 76.
2. See below, Chapter 1.
3. George Orwell, *Rebelión en la granja* (México: Promexa, 1987), 43. The prologue is omitted in most English editions.
4. Russell Jacoby, *The Last Intellectuals: American Culture in the Age of Academe* (New York: Noonday Press, 1993).
5. Jacoby, *The Last Intellectuals*, 6.
6. Jacoby, *The Last Intellectuals*, 8.
7. Jacoby, *The Last Intellectuals*, 12-14.
8. Jacoby, *The Last Intellectuals*, 15.
9. On the 1968 student movement, see: Herbert Braun, "Protests of Engagement: Dignity, False Love, and Self-Love in Mexico during 1968," *Comparative Studies in Society and History*, 39 (July 1997).
10. Enrique Krauze, "Jóvenes de ayer," *Siglo 21* (September 1993).
11. To commemorate Independence day, every year on September 15 at midnight, the Mexican president appears in the balcony of the presidential palace in the main Plaza of Mexico City, and shouts (*grito*) the name of several heroes of the revolution. He finally shouts *Viva México!*
12. Krauze, "Jóvenes de ayer."
13. Luis González de Alba, *Los años y los días* (México: ERA, 1975). For other witnesses' accounts, see also: Elena Poniatowska, *La noche de Tlatelolco* (Mexico: ERA, 1973).
14. Roger Bartra, "La república de las letras muertas y la muerte de las letras públicas," in *Oficio mexicano* (México: Grijalbo, 1993), 45-51.
15. Bartra, "La república de las letras muertas y la muerte de las letras públicas," 49.
16. Carlos Monsiváis, "No por mucho madurar amanece más temprano," *La Cultura en México*, no. 708 (September 1975).
17. Jorge G. Castañeda, *La utopía desarmada: Intrigas, dilemas y promesa de la izquierda en América Latina* (Mexico: Joaquín Mortiz/Planeta, 1993), 224-225.
18. Castañeda, *La utopía desarmada*, 224-225.
19. José Joaquín Brunner, *Educación superior en América Latina: cambios y desafíos* (México: Fondo de Cultura Económica, 1990), 74.
20. Castañeda, *La utopía desarmada*, 226.

21. Enrique González Pedrero, "Las enseñanzas del Fondo," in Cristina Pacheco, *Testimonios y conversaciones* (Mexico: Fondo de Cultura Económica, 1984), 100-101.

22. González Pedrero remembers of his teacher, "he loved German and French culture, and introduced us to some of its branches, in philosophy of law, sociology, theory of government, and literature, but always without neglecting the Greek and Latin classics." Alejandro Toledo and Pilar Jiménez Trejo, *Creación y poder: Nueve retratos de intelectuales* (Mexico: Joaquín Mortìz, 1994), 128.

23. Jacoby, *Last Intellectuals,* 117. See also: Todd Gitlin, *The Sixties: Days of Rage, Days of Hope* (New York: Bantam, 1987).

24. Russell Jacoby, *Dogmatic Wisdom: How the Culture Wars Divert Education and Distract America* (New York: Doubleday, 1994), 160-192.

25. Christopher Lasch, "Academic Pseudo-radicalism. The Charade of 'Subversion,'" in *The Revolt of the Elites and the Betrayal of Democracy* (New York: Norton, 1995), 176-197.

26. Castañeda, *La utopía desarmada,* 227.

27. Castañeda, *La utopía desarmada,* 227.

28. Monsiváis, "No por mucho madurar amanece más temprano," *La Cultura en México*, no. 708 (September 1975).

29. Jacoby, *Last Intellectuals,* x.

30. Thus the title of one of the few books on Mexican intellectuals. Roderic Ai Camp, *Los intelectuales y el Estado en el México del siglo XX* (Mexico: Fondo de Cultura Económica, 1995).

31. Enrique Krauze, "Los intelectuales y el Estado: la engañosa fascinación del poder," *Proceso*, no. 1005 (February 1996).

32. Krauze, "Los intelectuales y el Estado: la engañosa fascinación del poder."

33. Ricardo Pozas Horcasitas, "El pensamiento social francés en la sociología mexicana," *Revista Mexicana de Sociología*, no. 4 (1994): 314-315.

34. Horcasitas, "El pensamiento social francés en la sociología mexicana."

35. T.N.: a conservative party.

36. *La Cultura en México* was a weekly cultural review published in the magazine *Siempre!* during the seventies.

37. It remains to be seen if the Internet and other technological innovations, now making in-roads in Mexican society, will further critical thinking or not among millions of people.

38. Like Theodor Adorno, Hannah Arendt, Leo Strauss, and other European exiles in the United States, Spanish philosophers brought to Mexico new theories and approaches.

39. Luis Villoro, *En México, entre libro: Pensadores del siglo XX* (Mexico: Fondo de Cultura Económica, 1995).

40. Jacoby, *Last Intellectuals*, 219-220.

41. Peter Brimelow, *Alien Nation: Common Sense About America's Immigration Disaster* (New York: Random House, 1995).

42. Gary Dorrien, *The Neoconconservative Mind: Politics, Culture and the War of Ideology* (Philadelphia: Temple Univ. Press, 1993).

43. Michael Lind, "The death of intellectual conservatism," *Dissent* (Winter 1995): 42-47.

44. Lind, "The death of intellectual conservatism," 45.

45. Monsiváis, "No por mucho madrugar," v.

46. The survey was carried out in January 1995 at the Metropolitan Book Fair by the Alternativas Profesionales en Mercadotecnia (Professional Alternatives in Marketing) company. The sample taken was of 1,000 cases and the average age of those surveyed was between twenty-three and forty years.

47. Carlos Rubio Rosell, "Industria Editorial en Europa y México," *El Ángel*, 28 January 1996.

48. Rosell, "Industria Editorial."

49. Catherine Barr, ed., *The Bowker Annual: Library and Book Trade Almanac* (New Jersey: R.R. Bowker, 1995), 512.

50. Lasch, *Revolt of the Elites*, 170-171.

51. Lasch, *Revolt of the Elites*, Yet, it must be noted that at the time women and minorities had no right to vote and most immigrants and poor workers also were excluded from the political process.

52. Lasch, *Revolt of the Elites*, 163-164.

53. Luis Villoro, "La cultura mexicana de 1910 a 1960," in Villoro, *En México*, 10.

54. See below, chapter 1. Also see: Enrique Krauze, *Caudillos culturales de la Revolución Mexicana* (Mexico: Tusquets, 1999).

55. Krauze, *Caudillos culturales de la Revolución Mexicana*, 22-27.

56. Krauze, *Caudillos culturales de la Revolución Mexicana*, 34.

57. François-Xavier Guerra, *Modernidad e independencias: Ensayos sobre las revoluciones hispánicas* (Mexico: Fondo de Cultura Económica/Mapfre, 1992), 26-27.

58. Jaime Sánchez Susarrey, *El debate político e intelectual en Mexico* (México: Grijalbo, 1993), 30.

59. Pablo González Casanova, *La democracia en México* (México: Grijalbo, 1965).

60. For more on this, see José Antonio Aguilar Rivera, "Las razones de la tormenta: violencia y cambio político en México," *Nexos*, 19 (1996): 63-73.

61. See Maarten Van Delden, "The War on the Left in Octavio Paz's *Plural* (1971-1976)," *Annals of Scholarship*, 11 (1996): 133-157.

62. Octavio Paz, "Aclaraciones y reiteraciones," *Proceso* (January 8, 1978).

63. Carlos Monsiváis, "Rectificaciones y relecturas: y sin embargo lo dijo," *Proceso* (Jan. 9, 1978).

64. Enrique Semo, "El mundo desolado," *Proceso* (Oct. 25, 1978).

65. Carlos Monsiváis, "Interrelación cultural entre México y Estados Unidos," in *Mitos en las relaciones México-Estados Unidos*, ed. María Esther Schumacher (Mexico: Secretaría de Relaciones Exteriores/Fondo de Cultura Económica, 1994), 441.

66. Monsiváis, "Interrelación cultural entre México y Estados Unidos," 456.

67. Paul Hollander, "Mexican and Canadian Intellectuals," in *Anti-Americanism, Irrational and Rational* (New Brunswick: Transaction, 1995), 411-442.

68. Krauze, "Intelectuales y el Estado," 20.

69. See, for example, Edward Shils, *The Intellectuals and the Powers and Other Essays* (Chicago: The Univ. of Chicago Press, 1972).

70. For a sample, see I. Maclean, A. Montefiore, and P. Winch, eds., *The Political Responsibility of Intellectuals* (Cambridge: Cambridge Univ. Press, 1990); Antonio

Gramci, *La formación de los intelectuales* (Mexico: Grijalbo, 1967); Julien Benda, *The Treason of the Intellectuals* (New York: Norton, 1969); L. Fink, S. T. Leonard, and D. M. Reid, eds., *Intellectuals and Public Life: Between Radicalism and Reform* (Ithaca, N.Y.: Cornell Univ. Press, 1996).

71. Susarrey, "El debate," 73.

72. Octavio Paz, "La conjura de los letrados," *Vuelta*, no. 185 (April 1992).

73. Lasch, *The Revolt of the Elites*, 1-21.

74. Russell Jacoby, *Dogmatic Wisdom*, 14.

75. Kent Greenwalt, *Fighting Words: Individuals, Communities, and Liberties of Speech* (Princeton: Princeton Univ. Press, 1995).

76. Lasch, *The Revolt of the Elites*, 20-21.

77. David M. Ricci, *The Tragedy of Political Science, Politics, Scholarship, and Democracy* (New Haven: Yale Univ. Press, 1984), 65, 224.

78. For a sample, see: Benjamin R. Barber, *An Aristocracy of Everyone: The Politics of Education and the Future of America* (New York: Oxford Univ. Press, 1993); David Bromwich, *Politics by Other Means: Higher Education and Group Thinking* (New Haven: Yale Univ. Press, 1992); David Damrosh, *We Scholars: Changing the Culture of the University* (Cambridge. Mass.: Harvard Univ. Press, 1995); Bill Readings, *The University in Ruins* (Cambridge, Mass.: Harvard Univ. Press, 1996).

79. Richard Hofstadter, *Anti-Intellectualism in American Life* (New York: Vintage Books, 1963), 20.

80. Gabriel Zaid, *De los libros al poder* (Mexico: Grijalbo, 1988), 15-28.

81. Gilberto Guevara Niebla and Eduardo Mancera, "El desempeño educativo en América del Norte. Evaluación del aprendizaje en siete grandes ciudades," *Educación 2001*, no. 3 (August 1995): 18-23.

82. Gilberto Guevara Niebla et al., "Un diagnóstico global," in Gilberto Guevara Niebla, comp., *La catástrofe silenciosa* (México: Fondo de Cultura Económica, 1992), 32.

83. Guevara Niebla et. al., "Un diagnóstico global."

84. Allan Bloom, *The Closing of the American Mind* (New York: Simon and Schuster, 1984). The book was published in Spanish as: *El cierre de la mente moderna* (Barcelona: Plaza y Janés, 1989).

85. Bloom, *The Closing of the American Mind.*

86. Bloom, *The Closing of the American Mind,* 195.

87. Richard Rorty, "That Old-Time Philosophy," *The New Republic* (April 4, 1988): 28-33.

88. Harvey Mansfield Jr., "Democracy and the Great Books," *The New Republic* (April 4, 1988): 36.

89. Delal Baer, "Lo que es ser mexicanólogo," *Reforma*, 14 July 1995.

90. "Tlatoanis " were pre-Hispanic leaders who commanded a great amount of power.

91. Enrique Krauze and Héctor Aguilar Camín, "De los personajes," *La Cultura en México*, no. 548 (August 1972).

92. Jorge García-Robles, *La bala perdida: William S. Burroughs en México (1949-1952)* (México: Ediciones del Milenio, 1996).

Part Two

Chapter 3

Pilgrims at the Crossroads

I am not at the crossroads;
to choose
Is to go wrong.

Carlos Fuentes

"The image of my father standing with one foot in Mexico and the other in the United States," recalls Carlos Fuentes (1928) in his CBC Massey Lectures of 1984, "became a picture of my own self, a symbol of my imagination."[1] Such an imaginary is all too rare in late twentieth-century Mexico. After the death of the poet and Nobel laureate Octavio Paz in 1998, Fuentes is the last Mexican intellectual to exhibit such an openness.[2] Mexico has sealed itself markedly in the last fifty years. Ever more introverted, its intellectuals have turned to one another for comfort in the wake of a failed revolutionary nationalism and above all in the unfulfilled promises of modernity. "Lo mexicano," or Mexican exceptionalism, undertheorized and unreflective, prevails in this arena, with the more cosmopolitan intellectuals finding themselves at odds with their peers. In one of his most recent books, *The Crystal Edge* (*La Frontera de cristal*), Fuentes has one of the characters utter, "There are millions of migrant workers in the United States and thirty million people speak Spanish in that country. In turn, how many Mexicans can speak English correctly?" The novelist's alter ego responds: "Dyonisus only knows of two, Jorge Castañeda and Carlos Fuentes; and because of this they are suspicious."[3] Likewise, Paz complained that a certain ideological distrust had transformed him into "a suspicious personage and an exile in my own country." Regarding the contemporary Mexican intellectual world, Paz only stated that "for my generation and our elders, different questions interested us."[4] In *Myself with Others*, his intellectual biography published only in English, Fuentes wrote, "I am Mexican by will and imagination."[5] Simultaneously, another writer, Carlos

75

Monsiváis, spoke with disdain about younger Mexicans, in terms that would
have made Paz and Fuentes blush. "They are the first generation of Americans
born in Mexico." Between Fuentes and Monsiváis, there is more than a generational difference; there is also a difference of imaginary. Or as Fuentes
would say, of worlds imagined.

   The intellectual worlds of Mexico and those of the United States rarely
engage in direct dialogue; the appearance of *Myself with Others* produced that
rare moment. In June 1988, *The New Republic* published a very critical essay
on Fuentes in the guise of a book review.[6] The author of that review was
another Mexican, Enrique Krauze, historian and deputy director of *Vuelta* (1976-
1998), a highly influential monthly that was headed by Octavio Paz until his
death. As was later revealed, the essay had been commissioned to Krauze
explicitly by the editors of *The New Republic*. The article was published
simultaneously in both countries and immediately generated a great polemic.[7]
Many intellectuals of the left in Mexico felt compelled to come to the aid of
Fuentes. To this day, the topic still provokes strong opinions and the question
remains: Why Fuentes? Why Krauze? and Why in the United States? This
chapter traces the intellectual and political roots of the debate in the United
States and Mexico that ensued after the "review" by Krauze. In the critical essay,
Fuentes was taken to task for allegedly espousing a false nationalism. Ironically, Krauze's critics levelled the same charge against him, that by attacking a
national literary icon, Krauze was serving the interests of the American right.

The Case against Fuentes

   The polemic against Carlos Fuentes has a long history. In the memory and
consciousness of the U.S. public, it can de dated back to the 1960s and the
opposition to the Vietnam War. Fuentes has been a fierce critic of U.S. foreign
policy, first in Southeast Asia and later in Central America. American intervention in Cuba, Guatemala, Panama, Haiti, and Nicaragua dates back to the turn
of the century. In the 1980s, he publicly supported the Nicaraguan revolution
and was very critical of the policies of the Ronald Reagan administration
toward this Central American republic. In Mexico, the polemic arose out of his
open support for the presidency of Luis Echeverria (1970-1976). Alongside
Fuentes, many on the left, such as the anthropologist Fernando Benítez and the
novelist Ricardo Garibay, saw in Echeverria a successor to Lázaro Cárdenas,
arguably the most influential and popular president of the twentieth century.
The convergence begins here. With one foot in Mexico, where he lived, and
another in the United States, Fuentes wrote in 1972 a long article in *Plural*,
the predecessor to *Vuelta*, arguing that, "In the United States, a great historic
confrontation was taking place between the full exercise of civil liberties and

their negation by the military-industrial complex."[8] It was a presidential election and he was happy to play a part in the process. In the Richard Nixon–George McGovern contest, he saw "the contradictions of U.S. history, masked by naive optimism and manipulated by powerful groups."[9] The seizure of the Democratic Party new forces "signaled a revitalization of the political and social life of the country." The principal challenge to American democracy was the at the time occupant of the White House, "Richard Nixon Custer," and his campaign against the internal invasions of the "reborn Sioux." For Fuentes, the message was clear: "most perceptive Americans fear that the re-election of Nixon will mean a war against these reforms." His partisan views were not new; they harked back to his childhood in Washington, DC, and his front row seat in the development of the "New Deal" under Franklin D. Roosevelt. In his biography, he recalled that "Roosevelt taught us to believe that the first thing was for the United States to show that it was capable of living up to its ideals. I learned then my first political lesson."[10] The childhood of Fuentes in the United States, perhaps, can account for Krauze's indictment "[Fuentes] was a *gringo* boy of Mexican origin."[11] The resemblance of this indictment with Monsivais' is not fortuitous.

The U.S. elections were also vitally important for Mexico, exclaimed Fuentes. "The re-election of Nixon," he warned, "also signaled the gravest threat for Mexico and for all of Latin America, in their long and dramatic histories as victims of aggression, mutilation and exploitation."[12] The corollary to this affirmation was a rhetorical question: "Would Echeverria, Allende or Alvarado Velasco continue to be tolerated? Or will they be deemed intolerable, as were Francisco I. Madero and João Goulart?"[13] His fears were justified in the case of Chile's Allende, which would fall before a military coup within a year. But Echeverria was not Allende.

The bulwark against the imperial aggressions of the Republican Party would be the "Third-Worldist" policies of Echeverria, who "is acting internationally in defense of the Mexican national state, ensuring its viability, existence and development." Without appropriate mass movements to contain U.S. imperialism, "the only and minimum line of defense rests with certain countries."[14] Foremost among these is Mexico, for "Echeverria has identified Mexico with the Third World, the world of the poor and the wretched, alongside whom we must fight." Fuentes saw the possibility, however small, of a different course of events if McGovern were to become president. In all likelihood, however, "Nixon would have another four years to combat with brutality and intrigue any moderately reformist regime in Latin America."[15] The disastrous McGovern campaign would leave an indelible imprint on many of the aspiring leaders of the Democratic Party, including a young Bill Clinton.

Some Mexican intellectuals took issue with the political claims coming from Fuentes. In an open letter in *Plural*, Gabriel Zaid asked pointedly: "That your points of view coincide with those of the government, does not make them less respectable, when made independently. None can reproach you because you use your fame to make them known, if you act alone and if these are truly yours. But how can you forget that you are in Mexico? For you are doing the handiwork of the president."[16]

In October 1968, the Mexican army, in Tiananmem fashion, killed many middle-class students gathered at a prodemocracy demonstration in Mexico's City Tlatelolco square. Those that experienced first-hand the government repression of students at Tlatelolco in 1968 had, for obvious reasons, a much more critical view of Echeverria. After all, he had been the Minister of the Interior at the time and many believe that he had orchestrated the offensive. In his *Mexican Tragicomedy*, the writer José Agustín, a member of this generation, baptized the Echeverria regime as a "fun house" (*casa de la risa*). One of the first accomplishments of his presidency, notes Agustín, was the seduction of Carlos Fuentes, who not only jumped on board but also actively proselytized in its favor, with such slogans as 'Echeverria or Fascism.'" Fuentes organized a reunion between Echeverria and "The Most Outstanding New York Intellectuals" and as "a reward was given the post of Ambassador to France."[17] The novelist claims never to have made such a statement, but it was obvious that such was the mood. Many of the 1968 generation would never forgive Fuentes' flirt with Echeverria. Enrique Krauze and Héctor Aguilar Camín, both members of the 1968 generation and at the time students at El Colegio de México (one of the most prestigious universities in the nation's capital), were present at another fierce government repression in 1971. A paramilitary group beat and fired upon unarmed peaceful protesters. The event was such that both Krauze and Aguilar Camín ran home immediately ("with the sound of gunfire at our backs") to write an article for *La Cultura en Mexico*, the cultural supplement to the weekly *Siempre!,* headed at the time by Fernando Benitez.[18] The explanation that Fuentes offered, "on June 10, 1971, all the forces of Mexican reaction plotted to set a trap for Echeverria," seemed to many strained, if not disingenuous. No one believed such an argument. Fuentes himself recognized that "the national skepticism, above all in young people, is very deep and sadly well-justified."[19]

Given the lack of dialogue between the intellectual worlds in the United States and Mexico, it is a bit puzzling that the editors of *The New Republic* would ask Krauze for a critical essay on Fuentes. Krauze, after all, was all-but unknown outside of Mexico. Additionally, he did not write in English. On the other hand, Fuentes was prominent in both countries. The unusual circumstances surrounding the episode raised quite a few eyebrows. For some Americans, particularly for critics, the fact that Fuentes was Mexican went unnoticed. A well-known conservative critic, Paul Hollander, provides us with a clue in *Anti-Americanism*, when discussing the Sandinista government's reception of foreign guests. Hollander identified Fuentes and William Styron as "important *American* writers."[20] Such a mistaken, although prevalent, assumption gives a context by which to better understand the Krauze essay. For all intents and purposes, Fuentes had been "naturalized" as a U.S. intellectual. But one with an additional advantage: being able to speak on behalf of the Third World by virtue of his origins. "By will and imagination," he had become a player in the ideological and political wars of the 1980s in the United States.

If Fuentes was a kind of Janus figure, with one face looking south of the Rio Bravo and the other surveying north of the Rio Grande, it is important to also understand him from an American perspective. "Revolution" and "Fuentes" are words that have always gone together: Mexico, Cuba, Nicaragua. Three revolutions, three way stations and sources of conflict with the country of his childhood. He grew up in the shadow of the "institutionalized" Mexican Revolution and over the course of his life became attracted to many of the dreams of redemption of the twentieth century: Cardenista ("the second wave of the Mexican Revolution"); Cuban; student movements of the 1960s; and Nicaraguan. In an article for *Holiday* published in 1962, he explained that "'Revolution' is a keyword that separates the American and Mexican characters."[21] These were the years of the Cuban Missile Crisis, in which U.S. warships blockaded the island and the world seemed on the verge of a nuclear war. Fuentes was quick to denounce the blockade in *Siempre!* "as an act of piracy without precedent."[22] In light of the U.S. midterm elections, he saw that the Kennedy administration was gambling on a "spectacular action" against Cuba. The Democrats had allowed the Republicans to push them to the brink of armed invasion. The military-industrial complex also supported the blockade, in part to hide the failure of the Alliance for Progress. In sum, the act was a "casebook example of the modus operandi of the U.S. 'power elite': the military and corporate nexus finding their most extreme form under the Republican Party and its total control over the mass media sets the agenda for the foreign policy of the United States."[23] Only the combined actions of the Latin American countries, concluded Fuentes, could force the Unites States "to accept, at last, a new global reality." His political opinions, dating back to the late 1950s, had caused him trouble with the U.S. State Department. In his own words, he "had been blacklisted by the U.S. government since 1959, during the tenure of [John Foster] Dulles and under the rubric of the infamous McCarran-Walter Law, which dated to the McCarthy period."[24]

The writings and proclamations of Fuentes provoked the ire of the U.S. Embassy in Mexico. Saxton Bradford, the Public Affairs liaison, informed the State Department in a cable dated November 29, 1962, that, "The tone of Fuentes' article in *Holiday* was clearly aiming to attract sophisticated Americans through its use of irony (this in contrast to his perverse bluntness in the Mexican media). He makes superficial and happy cultural comparisons, permeated by his pathological hatred of the United States."[25]

The U.S. government was doubly frustrated by Fuentes. First, because the writer took his case to the American people as an example of official ideological intolerance. As Fuentes himself states, "My experience convinced me that I should take advantage of the North American forums, participating in the public discourse and, in doing so, making the political evolution of Mexico and Latin America known, denouncing the errors of U.S. foreign policy against us, trusting the essential goodness of the U.S. populace and making a clear distinction between the people and their government, between the democratic tradition of the former and the repeated infringements by the latter, above all in its relations with Latin America." These ideas would be repeated often. Second, by making a "victim" of Fuentes, the State Department brought the novelist to the attention of many of the prominent liberals of the U.S. cultural and literary world. Some of the most important friendships of the author can be dated to this period and shortly thereafter. He met William Styron at a conference of U.S. and Latin American writers and artists in Chichén Itzá, Mexico in 1964. They would become close friends, traveling to Europe frequently and spending long periods in Mexico and in Styron's summer home in Martha's Vineyard, Massachusetts. "The stroll from the cottage to the post office became known to us as 'Kant's Stroll,'"[26] remembered Fuentes. Thirty years later, the two would be joined for a weekend gathering by President Bill Clinton and another former *enfant terrible*, Gabriel Garcia Marquez. A cycle in the history of Cold War prejudices came to an end that day in Martha's Vineyard.

Styron and Fuentes not only shared friendship, they also saw eye to eye ideologically. A staunch liberal, Styron opposed the U.S. government's actions in Vietnam and in Nicaragua. The Ronald Reagan administration supported the armed opposition to the Sandinista government, the "Contras," in Nicaragua. This issue became a highly polemic topic of national debate. "Together we penetrated territories held by the Contras in Nicaragua," recalls Fuentes. Together they shared "the pain, the sadness of Nicaragua. The hospitals full of children mutilated by U.S. arms." The respect and admiration for another was strong and mutual. "I was moved," stated Fuentes, "by the way that Styron understood Latin America, coming from a radically different world, that of racist Virginia, denier of the same flesh, excluder of other words, other ideas: the Anglo-centric universe out of which Styron emerged as a man of letters. I have always read him with great admiration."

Fuentes is a man of books and of friends. Styron is one good example, another is Norman Mailer. It can be said that the State Department brought the two together. Upon learning of the ban on his entry into the United States, Fuentes wrote, "I resigned myself never again to set foot in U.S. territory, land that I love, that nurtured me and where, now, more than ever, I seek to participate in the public debate by appealing to the people." His fame made the exclusion very troublesome for the U.S. government. In 1963, with the appearance of Fuentes' new novel, *The Death of Artemio Cruz*, Attorney General Robert Kennedy, against the wishes of Secretary of State Dean Rusk, extended to Fuentes permission to travel to the United States. "I was allowed to visit only the island of Manhattan and only for four days. What possible menace could I introduce in my suitcases that I could not get across through my writings?" Mailer greeted Fuentes upon his arrival in New York. "'What!' —exclaimed Mailer, as we crossed the wires of mental telepathy, nightfall, the granite and steel of the Hart Crane Bridge—You mean to tell me that you cannot even come to my house in Brooklyn? Well, yes: my grunts were, more or less, the paranoid imitators of Alice's Mad Hatter. Mailer was angry, madness, in English, it was a tender madness, interiorized, angry at his own country." Given the absurdity of the ban, "we were going to defy the authorities, he was going to take me wherever we wanted."[27]

A feeling that things were shifting rapidly and profoundly in American society prevailed throughout the visit of Fuentes to New York. The Civil Rights Movement saw Martin Luther King's March to Washington that year, Kennedy was assassinated in Dallas, and the baby boomers began to express their dissatisfaction with much of mainstream society. Fuentes would later look at this time and proclaim that his and Mailer's rebelliousness signaled, in part, "the birth of the Sixties." In the years that followed, Fuentes became identified with this period in U.S. history, for which he was both admired and reviled.

In the writings of Mailer, Fuentes saw "the epic of a nation masking its deepest insecurities with excessive displays of the hubris, power, greed, sexuality, and foreign adventures in countries totally alien and incomprehensible to the American mind, so confident that what concerned it concerned the rest of the world. Mailer knew the truth behind such self-deluded perceptions. His writing is a deep and heartfelt effort to capture the complexity of the United States."[28]

The friendship with Mailer would prove crucial in his efforts to strike his name from the U.S. government's "black list." In 1969, Fuentes was once again barred from entering the United States and appealed to the American PEN Club and its president, Mailer, for support. The move proved effective. As Fuentes narrates the course of events: "Mailer publicly denounced the offensive dementia of the law and how it actually hurt the United States in the guise of protecting it from the Red Menace. The matter reached the Senate and Senator William Fulbright took up my case, passing a resolution forcing the Departments of State and Justice to grant me entry into the United States whenever I wanted."[29] Thus, the novelist was "naturalized" and absorbed by the left-liberal cultural and political sector of America.

Fuentes and his American friends shared a distaste for much of the existing U.S. foreign policy. In social and cultural terms, they also shared many affinities. Nonetheless, foreign policy questions were of prime importance for Fuentes, for obvious reasons. He tapped into a U.S. intellectual tradition dating back to John Reed and earlier, that sympathized with popular movements in the Third World. Fuentes quickly became a transnational spokesman against American intervention abroad. Unlike other U.S. liberals, he could claim to speak on behalf of the exploited millions of the continent, by virtue of his origins, and in elegant and perfect English. Hence, Fuentes became a valuable asset for the liberal camp.

Mr. Fuentes, Are You a Fellow Traveler?

Much of the discontent and malaise that the name Carlos Fuentes stirs up in certain intellectual and political circles is largely a legacy of the divisive years of the sixties. Conservatives consider him a symbol of those times, full of its romanticism and irresponsibility. The support of much of the U.S. left for the Nicaraguan Revolution was viewed as nothing but a pretext to express their continuing disagreement with their country's culture and values. It is truism that the sixties were a time of social upheaval, protest, change, and defiance of tradition. For the many that participated in sit-ins and student protests, these years were a period aptly characterized as "days of hope, years of rage." A time for action: political, personal, and collective. For many activists of "the age of Aquarius," the course of events have turned out sadly. Complacency now rules, with selfishness and materialism winning over idealism. The apogee of this decline came with the Reagan era and the meteoric rise of "Yuppies."

Another truism is that the sixties have disappeared. Many have written the period's obituary. Nonetheless, great disagreement remains about the cause of death, with some conservatives even asserting that the patient is not dead at all but still alive and doing well. For them, the sixties "revolution" became "institutionalized." The rebellious youths (now older and no longer wearing tie-dyes) are now professors, journalists, and professionals but still just as disenchanted and critical of mainstream society as ever. It is little wonder that opinions diverge so greatly as to the legacy of the sixties. Liberals see the dream as over in contemporary society, while conservatives still cannot wait to get out of the nightmare.

Like most of the Cold War, U.S. ideological battles extended into the developing world. The Third World has been a prism through which liberals see their own country's failings, romantically admiring other social and political systems, argues Hollander, and with the firmest belief that these are better endowed in all the virtues which the United States lacks. Life is elsewhere for many liberals since America is rampant with consumerism, angst, emptiness, and cultural despair. Dreams of redemption, community, integrity of spirit, the dignity of sharing, and humility are strong as revealed by the intensity of support given to revolutionary movements, such as the Cuban and Nicaraguan.

This sense of malaise impressed Fuentes early on. In the *Holiday* article he told an apocryphal story in which two youths were talking. One of them, a Mexican, wished to Americanize himself, the other, a young American poet, desired to Mexicanize. He would tell the Mexican "never allow deep Mexico to change. Cultivate it so that when the American Dream comes tumbling down, we can turn to it for a fuller understanding of life and of death, guilt, defeat, collective life and collective responsibility, of grace and of beauty. Do not allow this Mexico to change, for the United States, with its complacency, utter ignorance of tragedy, provincialism of all outside its borders, shall shatter in half and will begin the pilgrimage from skyscrapers to a freer world."

But the pilgrimage had already begun. And the pilgrims found themselves at a crossroads. Or so it seemed. In 1987, Tom Carson wrote in *The Village Voice*, "Nicaragua has become the crossroads. So many wishes and issues have converged upon it. A renewal of the possibility of revolution."[30] Left-liberal solidarity with Nicaragua was, according to conservative critics, a form of symbolic revival of the ideals of the sixties. The alienation of many American critics from their own country was deep.[31] Many felt that their country was singularly hypocritical and destructive and had systematically failed in its promises of collective regeneration. Consumerism, careerism, and individualism had sapped the vitality and the larger sense of community, of social justice and real values (recall that over a hundred years earlier Tocqueville had warned of the dangers of "the tyranny of the majority"). As one American mournfully stated about Nicaragua: "those people have a solid sense of community, which Americans lack."[32] In sum, the attractiveness of Nicaragua was the flip side of the repulsion of U.S. society.

Not everyone agreed with liberal self-flagellation, and reaction, in a literal sense, soon appeared. In a way, this could not be otherwise, for nationalism, although draped in universal ideals, has always been a powerful force in American society. The Sandinistas understood and exploited liberal guilt and shame. They learned well one of the lessons of the Vietnam War: in the United States, public opinion plays a vitally important role in the formulation of foreign policy. Supporters of the Sandinistas, such as Fuentes and others, also recognized this lesson. In a telling statement, the Sandinista Minister of Culture, Ernesto Cardenal, explained: "Fuentes is our translator in the United States."[33]

The feelings of national shame, of the rejection of the dominant culture and the romantic projections onto revolutionary regimes that ultimately end up as repressive or intolerant, provoked great consternation for American moderates and conservatives. This was particularly so for a sector that shared many of the traditional goals of left-liberals, but was taken aback by the melodramatic and self-hating actions of a good number of their peers. Additionally, much of the counterculture movement was not interested in reforming U.S. society; they simply rejected it outright. Such movement could not be truly progressive.[34]

The weepings of nostalgic liberals from the sixties unsettled those who aimed at taking over the Withe House, not the Berkeley Administration Building. Nicaragua had become a deeply divisive issue for liberals generally. Nicaragua, not domestic social reform, had become the main issue for the left. Due to this fact, the Sandinista revolution provoked not only opposition from the right but also from some moderates who regarded it as the last contracultural fad. Fuentes came to be seen as lobbyist on behalf of Nicaragua, because of his weight and influence. He had the advantage of speaking like an American, he knew the idiom of U.S. political discourse—but was *Latin American*. An even greater advantage working in his behalf was his sophistication, charm, and erudition on behalf of others. As he saw it, he was defending *his people*.

As we have seen, the question of "authenticity" was one of the main themes of U.S. critics. Fuentes was important because he was authentic. No other U.S. social critic could speak with the authority of the novelist, an authority stemming from his origins. Liberals, thus, had in Nicaragua a *truly* popular struggle and in Fuentes a *true* spokesman and defender.

In 1983, Harvard University invited the writer to deliver the commencement address.[35] "You seem to have forgotten that your own republic was born out of the barrel of a gun," Fuentes scolded his audience. The argument was not new, but this did not make it any less effective. He appealed to memory: JFK and FDR understood that the United States could not and should not intervene in the affairs of other countries. He rejected the facile argument that all revolutions would end up in the Soviet orbit. There was no determined outcome to these processes and to insist upon them is to engage in ideological slight-of-hand. Adding, "We the admirers of your extraordinary achievements in literature, science, and the arts and of your democratic institutions, of your Congress and your courts, your universities and publishing houses, and your free press, we, your true friends, because we are your friends, will not permit you to conduct yourselves in Latin American affairs as the Soviet Union conducts itself in East European and Central Asian affairs." And asking, "Why is the United States so impatient with four years of Sandinismo, when it was so tolerant of forty-five years of Somocismo?"[36]

It is interesting that criticism of Fuentes and his actions on behalf of Central America would come from *The New Republic*, since the publication is somewhat difficult to place along the political spectrum. As one of the most influential weeklies in Washington, DC, and a political and cultural hybrid, it is traditionally lumped along with the *The Atlantic, Harper's*, and the *New Yorker* as well as others as part of the "East Coast Liberal Establishment." Younger than many of its peers, it was founded in 1914 by Herbert Croly, a progressive newspaper man.[37] Over the years, it has been liberal, socialist, Stalinist, neo-liberal, and neo-conservative. Its apogee came in the 1960s. Such important writers as Walter Lippman, John Dewey, Alfred Kazin, and Irving Howe have written for *The New Republic*. Today, its circulation is about 100,000 and the typical reader is white, male, 40-ish, college-educated, and upper-middle class. On the political spectrum, it can be placed halfway between *The Nation* (left) and the *National Review* (right). The publication was bought in 1974 by Martin Peretz, a disillusioned civil rights activist and a one-time professor of sociology at Harvard. Under his tenure, the publication began to slide ever more to the right on questions of race and foreign policy. Many in the liberal press tagged this shift as a betrayal to the weekly's tradition. But Peretz merely saw it as a search for the "vital center." In many regards, the publication still continues to be a decidedly liberal publication.

During the Reagan years, the Republicans capitalized on the open disapproval of the Sandinista government expressed in *The New Republic*. The term "Reagan Doctrine," which called for a heavy-handed policy toward insurgency movements in Central America, was coined by Charles Krauthammer on its pages and was quickly adopted by the administration. Nevertheless, its pages have also repeatedly supported Democratic presidential candidates. Peretz had been Al Gore's instructor at Harvard and he shared much in common with Bill Clinton's brand of social reform. *The New Republic* supported the Arkansas governor's candidacy for president early and vigorously. When the Democrats returned to power in 1992, the publication openly celebrated.

In a way, *The New Republic* can be said to represent the conservative wing of the Democratic Party. This sector advocates a drive for more "respectable" middle-class and centrist politics, and a much less open identification with gay, feminist, and other "minority groups." "White collars" and "hard hats," decisive swing votes, it was argued cared little for countercultural politics and minority "special interests." To win back this part of the electorate, it was necessary to reintroduce the values of hard work and personal responsibility—long monopolized by the Republican Party. In short, Democrats had to shed the image of weakness and disunity and bring a greater focus to domestic issues. This is where Nicaragua entered the equation, for Central America had become the symbol of opposition politics in an age of conservative hegemony.

The New Democrats sought to regain control of their party's agenda by challenging many of their peers on the issue of Nicaragua. The editors of *The New Republic* saw this willingness to openly critique one another as a sign of intellectual maturity. Peretz himself would recall that "this was a position for which we fought. In the United States, there is a certain stratum of intellectuals in search of a future paradise. Nicaragua was their last chance."[38] Nicaragua, thus, became a family feud for U.S. liberals as well. The right continued firm in its claim that the Sandinistas were a Soviet "beachhead" in the Americas and must be stopped.

Peretz wrote frequently on Nicaragua in the second half of the 1980s, affirming that it was a utopia "that filled the vast emotional emptiness left with the sequential disenchantment with the Soviet Union, China, Cuba and Vietnam."[39] In his eyes, many of the old activists literally ran down ιο Nicaragua in the hopes of reaffirming their beliefs and recharging their batteries. In a 1985 article, entitled "The Myth of Revolution," he criticized such romanticism. Like Vietnam and Cambodia yesterday, "Nicaragua today enjoys showers of praise from the same group of left-liberals or their spiritual followers. The same stories appeared about 'happy peasants,' 'ever rising rates of literacy,' 'simplicity,' and 'sacrifice.'"[40]

The transformations taking place in Nicaragua were not all U.S. liberal projections. If they were, such a large campaign designed to discredit events and changes would not have been necessary. The Sandinistas toppled a long-reigning dictatorship and sought to bring about a more inclusive and just society. At the heart of the matter was an idealism that sought to redeem its poor and wretched and develop a coherent plan for economic development. All along, the Reagan administration financed counterrevolution and slapped an embargo on the country. In this respect, the Central American country was truly seeking to forge a moral community in very difficult circumstances.

The New Republic published some very critical commentary on the Sandinistas. Robert Leiken, an independent liberal, wrote a critical essay for Peretz in 1984 and quickly became *persona non grata* in many American liberal circles.[41] This family feud often took the tone of a "zero-sum" game, signaling that the real problem was the lack of room for a position that was both skeptical of the Sandinistas and anti-Contra. *The New Republic* took sides in this war and offered no quarter. A particular strategy was to attack the revolutionary imaginary of left-liberals as safe, distant, and inauthentic. This was, historically, a sign of the fickleness of U.S. intellectual romances with revolutions in the Third World. They always turned out badly and degenerated, some slower others faster, toward the "dustbin" of frustrated utopias. Nicaragua was the hope of a revolution with a human face. And it was presented to the world as such.

In this context, Fuentes, the translator of revolution, came to be seen as irksome for New Democrats, although much more so for the Reagan administration and the traditional right. For New Democrats, such as Peretz and Robert Reich, a member of the editorial board and later Secretary of Labor in the first Clinton term, Fuentes represented an obstacle to the "maturing" of the party and the concomitant restructuring of the New Deal State. The authority of the novelist in U.S. liberal establishment, as already mentioned, came from his origins: a Latin American with memories of the New Deal. It was precisely this angle that *The New Republic* sought to attack. This explains why neither Peretz nor his associates wrote the essay on Fuentes and why they sought a fellow Mexican to proclaim that he was a *fake*.

In Praise of an Actor

Leon Wieseltier, literary editor for *The New Republic,* commissioned a review of two books, *Myself with Others* and *The Old Gringo,* by Fuentes from
Enrique Krauze. Krauze had been a public critic of the novelist since 1976 and
jumped at the opportunity. Many of the comments in the essay were not new,
as Krauze acknowledged. What was unprecedented was the amount of space
and attention given by a major U.S. publication to a Mexican writer. For
starters, the cover gave a clear idea of the article's purpose by presenting a
caricature of Fuentes sporting an oversized Mexican sombrero, a great big
Zapata mustache, and bandoleers strewn across his chest stuffed full of pen-
cils. The caption read: "Guerrilla Dandy: The Literary and Political Illusions
of Carlos Fuentes, Everybody's Favorite Mexican." It was obvious that the
editors saw more than a Mexican intellectual in Fuentes; they saw a major
player in opposition to the Reagan administration policies and cultural wars
taking place in the media and across major American universities.

The subtitle was equally revealing. The "everybody's" comment was in
reference to U.S. left-liberals and their enchantment with authentic, yet suit-
able *Others.* Krauze opened his comments with a quote by Henry Fielding:
"He speaks all of his words distinctly, half as loud again as others. Anybody
can see he is an actor."[42] This was the only English portion of the text, the rest
was translated by the weekly. Fuentes was an "actor" playing a "role," pre-
tending to be something other than what he truly was. That such a charge
would be leveled against a writer of fiction seemed almost perverse. Ready-
made supporters of the novelist thought as much and argued that he could not
possibly be accused of "falseness." Was it legitimate to measure fiction works
with the standard of history?[43] The thrust of the argument was that Fuentes,
"claiming credentials he does not have," consistently presented a distorted and
highly stylized rendering of Mexico before the American public.[44] The matter
over "credentials" was ridiculous, of course. For while Fuentes, with his considerable erudition, is not an academic, neither is the historian Krauze. He is
a public intellectual, like Fuentes, with no institutional affiliation. Of late, he
has also become a significant cultural entrepreneur.

More was involved than a mere book review in the essay. The question was
over the accuracy of representation. To Krauze, Fuentes was more than just a
novelist; he was an "informal ambassador" by virtue of his access to the American public. As such, he had a "responsibility" to present an accurate picture of
Mexico. Krauze found his depictions to be "frivolous, unrealistic, and, all too
often, false." The accusation of "falseness" was really the key in the indictment that Fuentes had not acted properly in his capacity. It also revealed a
deeper symptom: the cosmopolitan novelist was criticized for offering a skewed
image, when, in fact, the best course of action would have been to present

alternative views, accounts, and impressions. Krauze and his generation exhib-
ited neither the interest nor the ability to make themselves heard on par with
Fuentes across the Rio Bravo and this generated a great deal of frustration.
They were also constrained by the growing parochialism of the second half of
the century in Mexico.

The review was published simultaneously in the United States and Mexico.
In Mexico, it appeared in *Vuelta*, despite some reservations by its head editor,
Octavio Paz. Years afterward, Paz lamented having consented to its publication, despite his own opposition to the Sandinista government. "How could I
deny the deputy director of *Vuelta* [Krauze]," asked the poet, "the right to
publish a polemic article without falling into a contradiction." The matter was
resolved in the name of "freedom of speech."[45] A careful examination of the
two versions will attest to its provincialism. Despite having been commissioned by a U.S. weekly, Krauze's essay was full of nuances, allusions, and
other factors that revealed that it was intended for a Mexican audience. This
may account for the great deal of editing in its English version. In Spanish,
the title was "The Mexican Comedy of Carlos Fuentes," while in the United
States, it was "The Guerrilla Dandy." The title was intended to strike a chord
for readers of *The New Republic* of the self-deceptions of chic radicalism. The
label of "dandyism," evoked the ability and convenience of political positions
without consequences, of easy commitment. The term was also intended to apply
to a fair segment of left-liberals, uneasy with their social and economic position.

The thrust of the articles changed from one version to another. In *Vuelta*,
the version was longer and Nicaragua did not dominate the discussion, as it
did in *The New Republic*. The issue of "authenticity," which opened the same
in both versions, was more pronounced in the Spanish. The "omnipresence of
Fuentes in the mass media" skewed and confounded the truth. Americans did
not know, could not know, "as we know that Fuentes do not know." A sen-
tence captured Krauze's indignation "Fuentes' key is not in Mexico but in
Hollywood." Fuentes, Krauze charged, "became used to seeing Mexico not in
its own terms, but reflected in the American perspective. No Mexican would
assert, as Fuentes does, that 'the american world blind us with its energy: we
can not see us but *you*.'" The issue of "own terms" elicited an unusual mixture
of nationalism and intimacy. Is there something such as a patriotic lens through
which *true reality* must be seen? As Krauze well knows the trauma of territorial conquest has not vanished from the collective memory of Mexicans.[46]

"Fuentes' was not exactly a life in exile, but an uprooting whose abrupt
reversal in adolescence would leave a scar of ambiguity," explained Krauze.
The charge was serious for an intellectual must give accounts of his roots.
Moreover, he must give his past an intrinsic worth, explaining its determinacy
in some instances and not in others. The personal history of Fuentes explained
his "uprootedness." Using one of his heroes as a counterpoint, Krauze argued

that José Vasconcelos faced many of the same issues and questions as Fuentes, but with one big exception: he "had no such conflict over identity. Not only was he fortified by his native language, but also by the practice of Mexican culture and familial nostalgia of his country."

The neat dichotomy set up by Krauze of Vasconcelos-Truth and Fuentes-False is, to say the least, strained. In one of his last interviews, Vasconcelos asserted that he and his generation "sought universal culture. We were terrified by provincialism."[47] He would later add that, "In Mexico, during my early years there was no great teacher. The United States had William James, while we had no equivalent." The writings of his professor, Justo Sierra, likewise, looked outside of the country and had little to say about Mexican culture. One of Vasconcelos' most memorable pieces of advice was "Read Plato, Dante and Shakespeare and then again read Plato, Dante and Shakespeare." His slight of Mexican authors was notorious. In his defense, Vasconcelos argued that, "Our generation was universalistic. We were interested in ancient Greece; we did not know anything or hardly anything about the history of Mexico."[48]

The highly essentialized image of Vasconcelos that Krauze used to contrast with Fuentes would have surely been rejected by Vasconcelos himself. Krauze, on the other hand, is of a generation closed in upon itself, parochial. This explains some of the anger and frustrations with the more cosmopolitan Fuentes. Defense of Mexican "tradition" and of "culture" could not have been farther removed from the spirit of the generation of Vasconcelos. *The New Republic* edited out the sections on Vasconcelos, probably because it smelled like "dirty laundry" among Mexican intellectuals and did not hold much interest for its American readers.

The criticism coming from Krauze toward the novelist was paradoxical. He accused the writer of propagating a primitive nationalism: "The only early links between Fuentes and his 'paternal country', were a nationalism forged less by pride in the Mexican tradition than by a resentment of the North American world, and by the determined effort he made throughout his childhood to preserve Spanish as his language."[49] It follows, then, that an upbringing characterized by "pride in Mexican tradition" would have led to a more enlightened and less reactive nationalism. A curious proposition. Krauze attacked the nationalism of Fuentes from an equally nationalist position. The historian was assertive in his defense of the "real" Mexico, which was precisely why he was approached by *The New Republic*. Primordialism assumes that origins can account for deeper forces. Native authenticity immunizes one against ideological confusion and allows for a clarity in judgment that outsiders, including the uprooted, cannot master.

Fuentes' background, explained Krauze, gave him "all of the advantages: before other writers, he was a natural cosmopolitan; before other cosmopolitans, he had the avidity to appropriate the 'imaginary imagined country.'" An "avidity" removed from the sources of authentic national identity: "[Fuentes] never understood the country, which served as the central theme of his work." The static qualities of understanding deployed by the historian stand out, as if childhood experiences prevented later discovery. Fuentes, no matter what, would continue to be a stranger in his land, unable to unlock the true mysteries of Mexican identity.

The leftist reaction in Mexico to the article was fierce. Some small hope existed that the publication would lead to a serious discussion over Fuentes' work, but was quickly dashed when Krauze was branded in the media as a traitor, reactionary, envious, Yankee stooge, and a mercenary. A few sympathizers argued that such vilifications were "easy, irrational, and illegitimate and failed to meet the author on his own terms."[50]

If the United States was in a war of position, culturally and politically, Mexico was caught in a struggle over loyalties. People took sides in the debate and a strong provincialism emerged. This was true not only of the nationalist critics of Krauze but also of the article, which itself highlighted the narrowing of cultural outlooks. Fuentes' "imagined imaginary country" might indeed be "false." The real question, however, is why should it trouble the likes of Krauze and other "authentic" Mexicans so? The answer was that Fuentes had a privileged access to the U.S. public and media. This privilege came, in part, because he was in a field by himself, with no other competing claims from fellow countrymen. One can share some of Krauze's misgivings without his sense of indignation. The real problem was not Fuentes, it was the failure of Krauze and his generation to compete more aggressively in the U.S. marketplace of ideas. It is not the job of Fuentes to represent the great diversity of Mexican intellectual opinion. That is for others. The animosity and the sensibilities of his critics pointed inward. Fuentes provoked suspicion, jealousies, and distrust in a world of conformity. Is it any wonder that he feels somewhat ill at ease in his own country?

The recent and well-received appearance of *Biography of Power* by Krauze appears to be a good step toward breaking down some of the intellectual isolation.[51] Still in contrast to Fuentes, Krauze cannot speak to his American readers directly. The translator of the book is as responsible for the success of the work as is the author. An important lesson seems to have been understood: it is imperative to be heard on the other side of the Rio Bravo. May others follow in his footsteps.

The Remains of a Controversy

The harsh words expressed by Krauze in 1988 were not forgotten. Eight years afterward, the incident reappeared in a series of exchanges initiated by Victor Flores Olea. Mexico emerged from the "lost decade" of the 1980s with great hopes of finally becoming part of the First World under the ambitious and dynamic leadership of Carlos Salinas de Gortari (1988-1994). Election year 1994, however, proved to be one of the most turmoiled in the nation's history: the official candidate of the ruling party, Luis Donaldo Colosio, was assassinated as was the head of the party. A massive currency devaluation took place shortly after the new president, Ernesto Zedillo, took office in December, in which the peso lost one-half its value. The Zapatista uprising in Chiapas was still unresolved. And violence seemed more pervasive in the apparent decomposition of the ruling party. One year into his term, Zedillo was criticized by Fuentes in a long commentary in *Proceso* in the following terms: "The general opinion is that he lacks historical vision and the political ability to confront the challenge at hand: an economic, political, moral, and historical crisis."[52]

Victor Flores Olea, a leftist intellectual, diplomat, photographer, and ex-government functionary, joined Fuentes in criticizing contemporary politics. As the former director of the Faculty of Social and Political Sciences at the National University in Mexico City as well as the National Council for Culture and Arts (Conaculta) under President Salinas, Flores Olea was a notable figure. It was widely rumored that he was sacked from Conaculta because of behind-the-scenes politics following his sponsorship of a "Winter Colloquium," which gathered Mexican and foreign intellectuals linked with the monthly *Nexos*. This angered the group associated with *Vuelta*, who had organized a similar event without Conaculta financial backing the previous year entitled, "The Experience of Liberty." Octavio Paz, the editor of *Vuelta*, was said to have come to Salinas and pressed for the ouster of Flores Olea. Once out of a job and with the declining fortunes of the Salinas administration, Flores became quite outspoken. Statements began appearing, such as "The Salinas administration, on the whole, could not have been more disastrous: on this a rare unanimity exists."[53] Paz was not spared either from public accusations, and he responded quickly in his magazine.[54] Krauze joined in the defense and asked, "Why did you, Flores Olea, serve in a government that sponsored colloquia so as to 'take conscience' of its own failings? If you had not been fired, wouldn't you still be there?"[55]

If at any moment, Mexican intellectuals appreciated clarity and lucidity in the discussion of ideas, now what counted was the sharpness of attack and the venting of spleen. Such was the level of debate in Mexico of things intellectual, cultural, and/or political. Flores Olea did not see a true exchange of ideas taking place, as he distrusted Paz for both his actions and denials. The same "disingenousness," he cried, was at work when Paz agreed to publish the vicious broadside against Fuentes by Krauze. All was done in the name of the "liberty of expression." "Was he unaware that Krauze was bought, they also looked elsewhere for other mercenaries—by people associated with *The New Republic* in a vain attempt to discredit Carlos Fuentes, a thorn on the side for the Reagan administration because of his defense of Nicaragua and Latin

America? How then can the editor of *Vuelta* explain away such a servile attack, on the friend in question, as freedom of speech? Where was the smallest shred of loyalty?"[56]

Flores Olea's claims made explicit what everyone knew implicitly: in Mexico the independence of intellectuals comes second to friendship within the small groups, that conflicts are over loyalties and not ideas, and that violators will face swift reprisals. The debate also revealed a deep ignorance of the inner workings of the American publishing and intellectual worlds. In 1994, Flores Olea published a book with the following comments on U.S. cultural influence in Mexico: "Consumer culture is not only the 'enemy' of Mexican 'identity' but of culture *tout court*. In other words, it also eats away at that great portion of American culture critical of the entertainment industries." The cure, as he saw it, was to "forge links between Mexican institutions and intellectuals with the 'sources' of great culture and art in the United States."[57] Where were these "sources" was never specified. It was evident that Flores Olea operated with a very abstract understanding of the United States, short on specifics and subtlety. His enemies were quick to seize these shortcomings.

Vuelta then published a letter from Leon Wieseltier, the literary editor of *The New Republic*, stating that, "He loved knowing that the article still keeps the apologists of Fuentes up at night, but saddened to see the vulgarity and ignorance of their responses." Wieseltier continued, "Flores Olea does not know anything about the origins of Krauze's essay or about the nature of U.S. intellectual life. I did not 'buy' the article: I paid for it." "Flores Olea overestimates his hero. The defense of Fuentes of the Sandinistas, not 'his defense of Nicaragua', as he states emphatically, does not appear to have posed a great challenge to U.S. foreign policy in Central America. There is no evidence that Oliver North reads Fuentes."[58] He added, "I asked Krauze to write the piece because I thought that Fuentes was a nuisance for the intellectual and literary world. That is my world."[59] The responses by the editor were sharp but overly simplistic given the history of the publication and the context around which it appeared. Without context, the essay appeared as an "ambush" in the eyes of many. "It may surprise Flores Olea," wrote Wieseltier, "to learn that in this country, and even in this city, writers are not mere lackeys of the White House."

What Wieseltier did, explained Flores Olea, was to commission an article to explicitly attack Fuentes because he considered him a "nuisance in the intellectual and literary world." "Is there a clearer example of the mercenary nature of the task?"[60] The supposed diversity of opinion of *The New Republic* "has not prevented it from being considered a mouthpiece for the most conservative thought in the United States. Krauze wrote on demand for an archconservative publication." He added, "I did not say that the article was ordered by the White House of Oliver North. But what about Elliot Abrams, Undersecretary for Latin American Affairs in the State Department, chief 'hawk' against the Sandinistas, and in charge of political negotiations in Central America? Has Wiseltier forgotten that Abrams is son-in-law to Podhoretz, the editor and intellectual force for many years at *The New Republic*?" Obviously, Flores Olea had confused Martin Peretz with Norman Podhoretz.

The U.S. intellectual world was foreign to Flores Olea and many others. Nonetheless, his responses yield significant insight into the politics of intellectual discussion in Mexico. The kind of "attack" described by the ex-director of Conaculta could only take place in tiny, closed quarters, where personal relations held sway over impersonal ideas. In a more plural world, differences and disagreements over ideas are depersonalized. There are also, simply, more positions, outlets, critics, and discussion. Personal loyalties, in such a world, are less pronounced and differences need not be as solitary. Between the extremes of denunciations and apologies lie an infinity of political opinions.

In the United States it is not rare for editors to select articles with certain authors in mind that these be paid accordingly. The pejorative "mercenary" used against Krauze by Flores Olea makes its impact because open public debate is so rare in a country like Mexico. In Mexican intellectual hamlets, fighting dragons and pursuing noble causes by unified bands of musketeers are the norm. Krauze said as much in one of his many defenses: "For Flores Olea, my essay was national treason, a sin worthy of the eternal fires of Hell."[61] After all as Wieseltier reminded, "The work of Carlos Fuentes is a topic over which decent people can disagree."[62]

The Mexican intellectual world is not "indecent," it is simply small. A vigorous exchange of ideas, the real measure of an intellectual community, cannot fully exist in Mexico until the public sphere expands and ultimately until tolerance and respect enter the national vocabulary. There is still too much passion and insufficient reflection. The Fuentes case points toward a way out of this dilemma: "a change of skin" or openness. Intellectuals, of course, do not operate in a vacuum. Cultures thrive on contact and exchange and die with isolation and neglect. "Each Latin American," affirms Fuentes, "will have a personal frontier with the United States." "And before the century ends," he adds, "each American will realize that he or she has a personal frontier with Latin America."[63] The question is: will each country's intellectuals be mute witnesses or active participants in this process? The signals appear mixed.

Notes

1. Carlos Fuentes, *Latin America At War With the Past* (Toronto: CBC Enterprises, 1985), 7.

2. On Carlos Fuentes, see: Jorge Hernández, *Carlos Fuentes: territorios del tiempo* (Mexico: Fondo de Cultura Económica, 1999); Raymond Williams, *Los escritos de Carlos Fuentes* (Mexico: Fondo de Cultura Económica, 1999).

3. Carlos Fuentes, *La frontera de cristal* (Mexico: Alfaguara, 1995), 69.

4. Silvia Cherem S., Interview with Octavio Paz, "Amistades y Enemistades," *Reforma*, 29 April 1996.

5. Carlos Fuentes, *Myself with Others: Selected Essays* (New York: Farrar, Straus & Giroux, 1988), 4.

6. Enrique Krauze, "Guerrilla Dandy. The Life and Easy Times of Carlos Fuentes," *The New Republic*, 27 June 1988.

7. Enrique Krauze, "La comedia mexicana de Carlos Fuentes," *Vuelta*, 12 (June 1988), reprinted in Enrique Krauze, *La historia cuenta* (Mexico: Tusquets, 1998), 187-220.

8. Carlos Fuentes, "Opciones críticas en el verano de nuestro descontento," *Plural*, 11 (August 1972).

9. Carlos Fuentes, "Opciones críticas en el verano de nuestro descontento."

10. Carlos Fuentes, *Myself with Others*, 4.

11. Enrique Krauze, "Guerrilla Dandy, The Life and Easy Times of Carlos Fuentes."

12. Carlos Fuentes, "Opciones críticas en el verano de nuestro descontento," 6.

13. Carlos Fuentes, "Opciones críticas en el verano de nuestro descontento," 6.

14. Carlos Fuentes, "Opciones críticas en el verano de nuestro descontento," 7.

15. Carlos Fuentes, "Opciones críticas en el verano de nuestro descontento," 7.

16. Gabriel Zaid, "Carta a Carlos Fuentes," *Plural*, 12 (September 1972).

17. José Agustín, *Tragicomedia mexicana 2: La vida en México de 1970 a 1988* (Mexico: Planeta, 1992), 17-18.

18. Héctor Aguilar Camín and Enrique Krauze, "La saña y el terror," *La cultura en México*, no. 490, 30 June 1971.

19. Carlos Fuentes, "Opciones críticas en el verano de nuestro descontento," 8.

20. Emphasis added. "A similar division of labor was evidenced during the visit of two important American writers, William Styron and Carlos Fuentes." Paul Hollander, *Anti-Americanism: Rational and Irrational* (New Brunswick: Transaction, 1995), 277.

21. Carlos Fuentes, "Latinos vs. gringos: algunas duras verdades," *Holiday* (October 1962), reproduced by *Proceso*, no. 972, 19 June 1995.

22. Carlos Fuentes, "¿López Mateos mediador? Dos caminos conducen a la guerra; uno a la paz," *Siempre!* 7 November 1962.

23. Carlos Fuentes, "¿López Mateos mediador? Dos caminos conducen a la guerra; uno a la paz," 56.

24. Carlos Fuentes, "Treinta años después," *Proceso*, no. 972, 19 June 1995.

25. "Para el Departamento de Estado, Carlos Fuentes era en 1962 sólo un engañoso escritor a sueldo, 'antiestadunidense y procomunista,'" *Proceso*, no. 972, 19 June 1995.

26. Carlos Fuentes, "Retratos en el tiempo," *La Jornada Semanal*, 21 April 1996.

27. Carlos Fuentes, "Retratos en el tiempo," 9.

28. Carlos Fuentes, "Retratos en el tiempo," 9.

29. Carlos Fuentes, "Treinta años después," 58.

30. Tom Carson, "The Long Way Back," *Village Voice*, 12 May 1987.

31. This is Hollander's argument, that captures conservative misgivings about liberal's stands.

32. Hollander, *Anti-Americanism*, 284.

33. "Fuentes has become deeply involved in the future of our country, as a Latin American, with a nationalist's continental conscience. And he has done so from the

entrails of the country that is attacking us." "Carlos Fuentes traduce a Nicaragua en Estados Unidos: Ernesto Cardenal," *Proceso*, no. 607, 20 June 1988, 47.

34. Lasch provides a poignant account of academic radicalism. Christopher Lasch, "Academic-Pseudo Radicalism: The Charade of Subversion," in *The Revolt of the Elites* (New York: Norton, 1995).

35. Fuentes, *Myself with Others.*

36. Fuentes, *Myself with Others.*

37. Walter Kirn, "The Editor as Gap Model: The New *New Republic* and the Politics of Pleasure," *New York Times Magazine*, 13 March 1993.

38. Kirn, "The Editor as Gap Model."

39. Martin Peretz, "Cambridge Diarist—Out of Line," *The New Republic*, 7 April 1986.

40. "The Myth of Revolution," *The New Republic*, 25 April 1985.

41. Robert S. Leiken, "Nicaragua's Untold Stories," *The New Republic*, 8 October 1984.

42. Krauze, "Guerrilla Dandy, The Life and Easy Times of Carlos Fuentes."

43. José Cueli, "Carlos Fuentes y la moral literaria," *La Jornada*, 3 July 1988.

44. Krauze, "La comedia mexicana," 15.

45. Octavio Paz, "La comedieta de Ponce," *Proceso*, no. 1003, 22 January 1996.

46. See, for instance: Julio Chávez Montes, *Heridas que no cierran* (Mexico: Grijalbo, 1988).

47. Emmanuel Carballo, *Diecinueve protagonistas de la literatura mexicana del siglo XX* (Mexico: Empresas Editoriales, 1965), 19-47.

48. Carballo, *Diecinueve protagonistas,* 19.

49. Emphasis added.

50. Hugo Hiriart, "¿Todos contra Krauze?," *La Jornada*, 24 July 1988.

51. Enrique Krauze, *Mexico: A Biography of Power: a History of Modern Mexico, 1810-1996,* trans. Hank Heifatz (New York: Harper Collins, 1997).

52. Carlos Fuentes, "En medio del desplome, la injuria de los crímenes y la corrupción," *Proceso*, no. 997, 11 December 1995.

53. "Flores Olea entra al debate: Paz, Córdoba y Otto Granados maniobraron para removerme de Conaculta," *Proceso,* no. 1004, 29 January 1996.

54. Octavio Paz, "Un Frégoli nativo," *Proceso,* no. 1005, 5 February 1996.

55. Enrique Krauze, "Cuatro preguntas a Flores Olea," *Proceso,* no. 1005, 5 February 1996.

56. Víctor Flores Olea, "Breve respuesta a un seráfico poeta y a un tartufo historiador," *Proceso*, no. 1006, 12 February 1996.

57. Víctor Flores Olea, *Rostros en movimiento* (Mexico: Cal y Arena, 1994), 35.

58. "Contestación del editor de *The New Republic* a Flores Olea: en Estados Unidos los escritores no cumplen encargos de la Casa Blanca," *Proceso*, no. 1007, 19 February 1996.

59. Emphasis added, Ibid.

60. Víctor Flores Olea, "Krauze o la condición del escritor mercenario," *Proceso,* no. 1008, 26 February 1996.

61. Enrique Krauze, "No le manden Flores," *Proceso*, no. 1009, 4 March 1996.

62. "Carta de Leon Wieseltier," in Ibid.

63. Fuentes, *Latin America at War with the Past.*

Chapter 4

The Present of an Illusion

It is ironic that today's Mexico is governed by a technocratic elite, trained in some of the most prestigious universities of the United States and most openly pro-American, yet who lacks a single intellectual spokesperson across the Rio Bravo. Despite the close and extensive ties between government officials and businessmen in both countries, the absence of an eloquent voice representing the neo-liberal modernizing project of the Mexican state is quite notable. The staff of specialists for each government is not up to the task, for it hardly ever reaches an audience beyond their respective ministries. In brief, there is no official equivalent of a Carlos Fuentes. The few Mexican intellectuals with a presence in the United States are, generally, of the left. Even more ironic is that those Mexicans best able to maneuver in the United States tend to be the most nationalistic and skeptical of closer relations between the two countries. This paradox is worth exploring in some detail.

Cosmopolitan Nationalism

Of the new generation of Mexican intellectuals, Jorge G. Castañeda (1953) has been the most successful in carving a niche for himself in the United States.[1] He is a regular contributor to the Mexican opposition weekly, *Proceso;* to the dailies, *Los Angeles Times, El País, Le Monde Diplomatique;* and to the U.S. weekly, *Newsweek.* In 1988, after an initial flirt with the candidacy of Carlos Salinas of the ruling party, he decided to cast his lot with the leftist democratic current, headed by Cuauhtémoc Cárdenas. Quickly he became one of the most vocal critics of the Mexican State and "the most vilified and attacked Mexican political analyst in recent memory."[2] This sudden notoriety was due to the fact that Castañeda had an audience outside of Mexico. The Mexican regime, obsessed with its image abroad, found the independence of Castañeda very uncomfortable. Frustrations increased as the government found it difficult to engage him in a serious discussion on his own terms and could not sway his opinions one bit. Efforts aimed at co-optation met an empty silence and a process of escalation began first with negative press and ultimately with veiled and even direct physical threats.[3]

Like Carlos Fuentes, Castañeda understands the keywords and subtleties of U.S. political discourse, where "liberty," "individualism," "opportunity," and "progress" speak of a national experience and a common destiny. This is a discourse that Mexican technocrats, despite their studies in the United States, still cannot master. The similarities between Fuentes and Castañeda are not coincidental. Both come from diplomatic families—Fuentes was friends with Castañeda's father in the Mexican Foreign Service. Like Fuentes, Castañeda also lived and studied in the United States. In the early 1970s, he "majored in economics and history [at Princeton University]." As he later recalled, "I was bored, finishing in three years my BA and headed for Paris. Really, my formative years were in Paris between 1973 and 1978."[4] There he obtained a doctorate in economic history at the Sorbonne. French intellectual society would leave a deep imprint upon him. There he met Fuentes and Regis Debray among many others. He became acquainted with the fashionable currents of Althusserian Marxism and deconstructionism. Upon his return to Mexico, he participated briefly in the Mexican Communist Party while his father served as Secretary of Foreign Relations under President José Lopez Portillo (1976-1982). Castañeda is no stranger to seeing power up close. In an informal but effective capacity, he contributed to the shaping of Mexican foreign policy in the early 1980s. "The entire peace process in El Salvador from its inception, initial negotiation to the actual signing of the French-Mexican Declaration," explains Castañeda, "was due to my efforts and those of Regis Debray. There was no guilt involved working with the government. First, I received no salary, no office, no secretary. This allowed for a certain detachment, a false one, but a detachment nonetheless."[5]

His experiences in France coupled with access to the highest levels of government at an early age profoundly shaped Castañeda. Born as part of an elite destined to rule, his ideological convictions and political inclinations led him to join the opposition. Nonetheless, even as an outsider, he continued to be very much an *insider*. His network of friends and contacts on both continents is enormous as is his prestige as a journalist, speaker, and academic. Both increased with his criticism of the Salinas administration (1988-1994) and the ensuing attacks against him. Like few other Mexicans, Castañeda moves like a fish in the water in both Mexican and U.S. cultural, academic, and political circles. Whereas most of his Mexican peers cannot utter the following lines, Castañeda can and has: "I earn a pretty good living as a leftist intellectual."[6]

Traditionally Latin American intellectuals have been ardent nationalists. In part, this is due to the fact that historically much of the labors of "nation-building" has rested on their shoulders. Since independence, their task has been to invent traditions, myths, and legends, accentuating the singularities and sculpting in the historic imagination the epic of the nation, its mission and destiny.[7] Thus, it should come as no surprise that many intellectuals are more nationalist than their countrymen, who are often less versed in the art of patriotic symbology and imagery. Paraphrasing Professor Benedict Anderson, communities are not imagined by themselves.[8] What is ironic, however, is often times those most exposed to the ideas of the rest of the world are often the most opposed to its diversity.[9]

In Latin America, explains Castañeda, it is usually the intellectual left that waves "the theme of nationalism and national sovereignty, often linking it to U.S. policy towards one country or the entire region, habitually in the form of intervention. The legacy of U.S. meddling in the internal affairs of the continent reinforced the conviction of many intellectuals that the United States for too long had deprived the countries of Latin America of their pride and sovereignty."[10] As memory speaks, it calls for obedience. History becomes, thus, a cliché, a trap imprisoning imagination and denying movement and transcendence. Only a few of the more sophisticated leftist intellectuals, such a Fuentes and Castañeda, make a distinction between state and society in the United States. Although, Castañeda exhibits more traces of that venerable leftist quality, anti-Americanism.

Around the time of the 1988 Mexican presidential elections, the prestigious publishing house Alfred A. Knopf commissioned a book from Castañeda and Robert Pastor on U.S.-Mexican relations. The book would be jointly authored by a Mexican of the left and an American well-acquainted with the bureaucratic establishment in Washington, DC. Pastor (1947) served in the Jimmy Carter administration (1977-1981), as director of Latin American Affairs for the White House National Security Council. With the Republican ascendancy in the 1980s, he returned to academia as director of the Carter Latin American and Caribbean Center at Emory University. He was a Fulbright Visiting Professor at El Colegio de Mexico for the academic term 1985-1986. The final product was called *Limits to Friendship: The United States and Mexico*.[11] It was only after the completion of the work that it dawned upon the authors to translate and publish it in Mexico. Although originally conceived for a U.S. audience, no substantive changes were made and the book appeared as such. A Spanish edition by the publishing house of Joaquín Mortiz y Planeta appeared a year later. It included a new preface and a change in the order of the authors and countries, revealing an underlying nationalism.[12] *Limits to Friendship* was conceived as an all-too rare binational dialogue of actual processes and events. The exchange by the authors was an important step in cultivating real discussion; but it also revealed some of the difficulties of bridging cultural differences.

"There is only one way to reduce the weight of U.S. influence," explained Castañeda in 1988, "and that is that we must understand and make the United States understand that better relations means less relations."[13] His suggestion was not very realistic for interdependence between the two countries had long since escaped the control of both governments. The legal and illegal flows of people, goods, investment capital, services, narcotics, weapons, and disposal of waste have increased exponentially between the two countries. A North American Free Trade Agreement (NAFTA) seemed like a pipe dream ten years ago as the candidate Salinas declared that such an agreement might not be in the best interests of Mexico. Nevertheless, informal integration proceeded quickly apace.

The collapse of communism in 1989 sent shock waves across the world, provoking deep introspection, doubt, angst, despair, hope, glee, and triumphalist celebration. Mexico was not exempt from this ripple effect, which also coincided with a larger crisis of nationalism. "We are not less nationalistic than before nor has our country become more pro-American," affirmed Castañeda. "What is occurring is that our nationalism is searching for new goals and new causes to defend."[14] Clearly, he was uncomfortable in having Mexican nationalism become an object of scrutiny. Nationalism was a question that divided Castañeda and Pastor. "In my opinion," argued Castañeda, "the chapters by Robert Pastor underestimate the power and vitality of Mexican nationalism, particularly its anti-American thrust . . . nothing can guarantee that Mexico will be more democratic, less progressive, less nationalistic or anti-American, actually, there are signs to the contrary."[15] Pastor acknowledged that Castañeda belonged to a "new breed" of intellectuals less inclined to blame the United States for all of the world's shortcomings. Nonetheless, he warned that "there is in his arguments an unmistakable undercurrent that the United States has much to do with the difficulties of Mexico."[16]

Pastor, in his analysis of the neighbor to the south, was right on the mark: democracy was crucial for a peaceful transformation in Mexico. Time would prove him right, for he believed that it was both possible to extend ties between the two countries and at the same time improve relations. Once NAFTA negotiations got underway, Pastor became one of its key supporters in the United States. In many ways, his support was an extension of a previous line of argument expressed before there was any interests either in Los Pinos or the White House. Pastor clearly saw many of the obstacles involved in bringing about such an agreement. If Mexico should suddenly export too much to the United States, it could trigger protectionist tendencies. Having overcome many of the national reticence in Mexico, NAFTA now faced great opposition in the United States.

In an effort to address concerns that NAFTA would mean a loss of jobs and a decline in U.S. salaries, Pastor wrote a small book in its favor.[17] When the Democratic Party returned to power in 1992 after a twelve-year absence, President Bill Clinton took up NAFTA, formerly a Republican project, and made it a bipartisan issue. The matter deeply divided the president's party and may have cost him his ambitious health care reform package. Key constituencies of the party opposed NAFTA: organized labor feared the loss of jobs; blacks and Hispanics a fall in wages and an all-together disappearance of blue-collar jobs; and middle classes a drop in their standard of living.

Pastor's counterargument was simple: U.S. economic problems were serious but economic isolationism would only worsen the situation. Americans could not afford the luxury of delaying much needed structural measures and changes. In the long run, if America was to be competitive and dynamic it had to continue further internationalizing its economy. The key was not to protect low-wage and low-skilled industries and workers, it was to make these sectors disappear altogether. This was easier said than done, particularly given the increasing economic inequality of the last few years that transformed parts of the United States into islands of Third World poverty and despair. There was also an ominous tone about the disappearance of entire industries and workers. Where would they go?

Populist opposition to NAFTA was headed by eccentric Texas billionaire, H. Ross Perot. In 1993, Mexico dominated political discussion in the United States as never before. The process quickly became a national spectacle and included a debate between Vice President Al Gore and Perot, which Gore easily won. Viewers, worried about the impact of NAFTA upon their livelihood, watched two talking heads debate one another, wielding few facts and easing few minds. Despite the televised defeat of the pesky Perot, who quieted down thereafter, the battle for congressional ratification was far from over. Big multinational firms lobbied hard for passage, since they stood to profit greatly with the reduction of tariffs. The very visible corporate support seemed to many Americans a symbol of both corporate and political corruption, arrogance, greed, and insensitivity in the face of the decline of major urban inner cities, increasing levels of violence and drug use, corporate downsizing, the disappearance of work, and the degradation of the environment.

Many U.S. left-liberals united in vocal opposition to NAFTA. Intellectuals, such as Noam Chomksy, published articles and pamphlets and toured the country denouncing the proposed free trade agreement as the latest strategy by the "masters of capital" to further squeeze the dispossessed.[18] In Mexico, contrary to predictions—including those of Castañeda—no mass nationalist reaction surged. Some sectors, such as the traditional opponents of American influence found on both the left and the right, did, indeed, mobilize and protest the accords but protest was far smaller than that found in the United States. José Angel Conchello, a longtime member of the conservative National Action Party (PAN), took up the banner, arguing that the asymmetries between countries would reduce Mexico to a mere consumer of American goods. The future meant a market drowned in "made in the USA" labels. Mexico would be transformed into a giant *maquiladora* producing intermediate goods at best and based on cheap labor.[19] Interestingly, such warnings and appeals to the historic legacy of U.S. imperialism in the country found small appeal compared to the intoxicating dream of joining the First World. Like the railroads of a century earlier, NAFTA would be the key to the promised modernity for Mexico. In some ways, the inability to jump start nationalist opposition may have contributed to the indigenous uprising of the Zapatista Army of National Liberation (EZLN) in the state of Chiapas *after* passage of the agreement. Launching a guerrilla strike after the fact made the movement seem fatalistic. It fired the revolutionary imagination in the country. It also was a clear signal that many pressing issues and conditions could not be dealt with peacefully through parliamentary means, since economic interests and politicians long since made a sham of the democratic process. Influence was bought and sold openly, with many finding themselves naked in the face of a new "savage" capitalism. Given the extreme structural inequalities and violence associated with regional chieftains, powerful landowners, and their band of mercenaries in Chiapas, there may have been no other option but armed revolt. The rest of the country sympathized with the plight of their fellow Mexicans, but considered NAFTA a much more promising long-term national solution than the taking up of arms. The absence of a more fervent nationalist outcry was a true revelation for many intellectuals.

In *Utopia Unarmed*, Castañeda sharply criticized the "sexy" and "romantic" imagery associated with guerrilla movements. The intellectual left, he added "adulates its victims" without really stopping to consider the exigencies of such costs. "This condescendence exhibits the weakness of their theoretical, political, even and even humanistic perspective: the miseries were real enough, but the gulf separating the analysis of intellectuals and the lived-experience of poverty was greater than ever." Intellectuals, "did not always grasp that despite the continuing or even worsening of inequalities, absolute gains were important for millions of the poor that previously had nothing and little by little began to acquire something."[20] This fact, explained why the revolution so eagerly awaited by intellectuals never came.

Castañeda, however, seems to have trouble following his own advice. In many regards, he is equally shortsighted and dogmatic as those he criticizes. Indeed, times had changed and the Mexican people, despite well-deserved reservations about the United States, were proving much more open about the future than many intellectuals. A poll taken in early 1991 revealed that 59 percent of Mexicans would be willing to form a single country with the United States if it meant an improved standard of living. Fifty-four percent claimed to be very proud of being Mexican with 56 percent stating that they would be willing to fight for their country in the event of a war. Seventy one percent believed that there should be no barriers to the free movement of goods and services across borders, with 57 percent expressing interest in expanding economic ties with the United States.[21] Along with other studies, a general pattern seemed to be emerging: nationalist feelings appeared to be declining, not only in Mexico but also in Canada and the United States.[22]

These poll findings, to be sure, need to be taken with a grain of salt. No firm conclusions could be drawn when measuring something so complex culturally and politically as "nationalism."[23] Popular opinion can often be fickle and contradictory. And there is always the problem of getting a representative sample of the population. A good example of the difficulties can be seen in a poll taken by the daily *Reforma* in 1995 to determine the range of opinions Mexicans held about the United States. Forty percent of those polled expressed either a "very good" or "good" opinion. Thirty percent had an O.K. view and only 27 percent said they had a "bad" or "negative" opinion. At the same time, 56 percent believed U.S. influence was excessive in Mexico, with only 11 percent arguing for an increased presence.[24] The apparently contradictory results could be summed up in the following manner: even a good neighbor, can at times, be too intrusive. Just as one could claim to see nationalist feelings declining, others saw them merely as latent, capable of rising again in Phoenix-like fashion.

The rise of pollsters and efforts to measure public opinion on contemporary issues seems to be undermining one of the historical roles of Mexican public intellectuals: to be the interpreters of civil society. This is part of a process of "secularization" in which "intermediary bodies," such as intellectuals, are eliminated and a much more direct form of public expression is allowed. Intellectuals, despite these developments, cling to their self-assigned role as spokespersons on behalf of the great "silent majority." They still addressed larger issues and questions as well as the need for structural reform that many ignored or downplayed. Such assumed "responsibilities" are understandable for they define the role of intellectuals.

It is often stated that intellectuals not only have the responsibility of interpreting their societies but also of forming them. This is true, if societies allow it, either negatively or positively. Public opinion polls locate society and its tendencies at the center of discussion, constituting a minor revolution in the traditional public sphere. What people "want" stops being a question of speculation and becomes an object of analysis. "Scientific" polling, with is "hard" data and tables, challenges some of the metaphysical qualities of the interpreters of the "general will." If "the people" do not necessarily speak in these polls, they at least whisper a good number of things. Intellectuals could either agree or disagree with public opinion, but one thing is certain: they are *not* public opinion. Slowly Mexican intellectuals begin to resemble their counterparts in other parts of the world. U.S. opinion polls measure shifts, trends, and outlooks in such minute and obsessive detail rarely seen elsewhere. Its intellectuals are aware of the likes of the American people, although they often reject them.

Mexican intellectuals had long acted as spokespersons for a people that did not speak. They often forgot that it was they who argued and debated and not civil society, as revealed by the shock of discovery that the country was less nationalist than imagined. These increasingly displaced spokesmen observed with a mixture of incredulity and shock, the passing of the torch. U.S. intellectuals do not share the same pious fiction of expressing the wishes of the larger society. And, increasingly they do not share many of the larger societal values, aspirations, and tastes, with a resulting process of estrangement and rejection.

In Mexico, the conflation intellectuals-society engendered a spurious romance. Its society is no less anti-intellectual than that of the United States. Although its intellectuals speak, they increasingly have trouble reaching the masses. The haze, caused by a listless social society, allows for an "imagined country" to exist, a melancholic, reflexive and hurt nation that is, nonetheless, heroic, generous, and burdened with memories. It is a place that never forgets, particularly historic wrongs. It is also a people than can do everything, except speak for itself. It whispers its secrets, wishes, and hopes in the ear of those who will listen in the hopes of making them known. Like in medieval times, chroniclers are necessary for a society that does not speak, but organizes. Above all, it is a people nationalist to the bone. Nationalism, never disappears from the hearts and minds of Mexicans, who cannot help but believe in the Virgin of Guadalupe and be anti-American, it merely rests. Whomever does not conform does not truly know Mexico. Or worse yet, is a pariah. Generally, however, he is just a victim of false patriotic conscience.

The intellectual left found it easier to discard with Marxist dialectics than to do away with their deeply engrained nationalist feelings. Unless, they become capable of dialogue, the gulf shall widen between them and the average citizen. A gathering of voices is what is needed at this juncture, not extended solos. Intellectuals need to understand this before they are left preaching in an empty temple.

Against Wind and Tide

Castañeda was the most visible Mexican opponent to NAFTA. Like much of the Mexican left, he saw the accords as a serious threat to national identity. Because of his very public influence outside of Mexico, he became a constant headache for the Salinas government, which sought every possible way to silence criticism. The reasons for Castañeda's opposition were not new; they had been put forth, in essence, years earlier in *Limits to Friendship*. While most Mexicans heralded the coming of a new age, Castañeda was forecasting gloom and doom, which made him stand out in the U.S. media. Like in 1989, he was arguing that better relations meant less relations. Without discarding free trade altogether, he criticized the false inevitability surrounding NAFTA and the specific terms negotiated. The accord on the table lacked many essential political, social, cultural, and ecological aspects. There was no vision as to how the process of integration would proceed beyond the gradual liberalization of certain goods and services. Fundamental asymmetries were not taken into account and Mexico entered as a very junior partner, without the privilege, means, or recourse to defend itself appropriately. Mexico could opt for other, and better, models of integration. It did not have to sign what was on the table, which was "highly dynamic, but anti-social, short-term and anti-interventionist and full of inequalities."[25] A "better accord" would be more along the lines of the European model, constructing supranational institutions and helping bring Mexico's society and institutions closer to those of the United States and Canada. Under the terms of this latter accord, there would be sufficient funds available to ease the costs of adjustment so that nobody suffered excessively. There would also be a trilateral industrial policy that would check some of the negative effects of the market. State intervention should be a basic principle of the regulation and planning of the economy. Other issues were to be included, such as the movement of labor across borders and workers' rights. Social issues needed to be a part of the accords as did environmental protection.

The fundamental problem with Castañeda's recommendations was that they implied a loss of sovereignty that no politician in either of the three countries involved could agree to publicly. The debate over NAFTA revealed that differences had widened between the former authors of *Limits to Friendship*. Pastor, despite sharing some of Castañeda's misgivings, became an ardent supporter of the agreement. He considered NAFTA a better deal than none at all, and was hopeful that some of the omissions could be corrected at a later point as integration broadened to include social questions. It was obvious, however, that NAFTA political fortunes in Washington, DC, would not survive a much more comprehensive and overly ambitious initial agreement. A compensatory fund would have little chance of passage at a time in which the New Deal welfare state faced an onslaught from all sides and when budget deficit reduction had become a national issue, spearheaded by Republicans. For many moderates, such as Pastor, the hope was that once signed and with the passage of time as well as decline of Republican fortunes, many needed adjustments could be made to the NAFTA accords. After all, the European Union (EU) was not forged in a single day. The signing of the agreement was only the first step of a long and complex historic undertaking.

With the ratification process reaching a climax in the autumn of 1993, an article appeared by Castañeda in the prestigious journal, *Foreign Affairs,* arguing against NAFTA.[26] The appearance of the essay was a landmark, for rarely had a Mexican author access to such a select audience. Published by the influential Council of Foreign Relations, the journal printed some of the most influential essays of the latter half of the twentieth century, such as George Kennan's famous "Mr. X" article heralding the start of the Cold War.[27]

"The accord," wrote Castañeda, "in itself involves great risks." His objections were well-known: the asymmetries of the two countries; the absence of compensatory mechanisms. This time, however, the emphasis was on the "premodern" condition of Mexico and in the incapacity of the trade agreement to alter this fact. Castañeda was putting forth the argument that democracy and economic liberalism did not necessarily go together. In the 1980s, one of the bleakest economic periods for Latin America since the Great Depression, economic liberalism made a return, arguing that if the "market" was only allowed to operate freely, it would eventually lead to democracy. This correlation was not new of course, but the unflinching faith in the regenerative powers of the free market was. Indeed, evidence seems to indicate that democracies survive better in sound economies. Many of the converts to economic liberalism saw free-market policies as an indirect means to achieve political reform. In Mexico, that seemed an attractive option since the challenge was to bring about reform within a deeply divided single party state, without appearing to be under the dictates of the United States or the International Monetary Fund and without triggering a nationalist backlash. Along the way, however, many government officials became more Catholic than the Pope in their zeal to deploy neoclassical solutions to the Mexican economy with singular vision and rigor.

Castañeda's *Foreign Affairs* article was written as a rejoinder to the neoliberal project and to the selling of NAFTA as the sole answer to Mexico's long quest for modernity. The accord could not, by itself, modernize Mexico. On the contrary, he added, "the short-term effect may well be to halt the impulses for political reform." According to Castañeda, NAFTA wrongly assumed that the three member countries had similar market economies. An agreement more along the lines of the EEC would be better. Additionally, democracy should be a *sine qua non* for membership. Not signing the accords did not imply the end of the world, as the Mexican government was auguring. It would have been a devastating blow only to the Salinas regime, which had gambled everything in the process. For the country, however, the decision not to sign would mean a further opening of the political and democratic process.

The ubiquity of Castañeda in the U.S. media and his message made him a celebrity abroad, while in Mexico he was depicted as a dangerous saboteur of national destinies. Passage in the U.S. Congress was not an easy affair, for it took all of President Clinton political muscle to round up sufficient votes. A massive campaign was launched in Mexico to discredit Castañeda and other critics. The passage of NAFTA in Mexico, given the authoritarian system, was already a done deal. Officialist newspapers and writers began to wield their knives against the "intellectual traitor" who spent his time bad-mouthing the country abroad. The attacks increased as Castañeda and another leftist intellectual, Adolfo Aguilar Zínser, agreed to present their views before a U.S. congressional committee.[28] Opposition to NAFTA in the United States made strange bedfellows as Castañeda found himself allied with left-liberals, organized labor, and also with populists of the right and xenophobes, such as Ross Perot and Patrick Buchanan.

The bitter and defensive political climate in Mexico foreclosed the possibility of a necessary debate on vital national questions. In the words of Castañeda, "an official lynching campaign was launched against those of us who speak the same here and abroad."[29] Vilification of opponents to NAFTA served to draw attention away from the absence of debate and the authoritarian nature of political power. Opponents to the accords also used their status as "victims" to deflect any and all criticism as "officialist," thereby not having to respond to legitimate objections, such as those surrounding the controversial statements of Castañeda. Nobody emerged a "winner" in this fight. Not the government nor the opposition nor the public at large.

After a long and bitter battle, NAFTA was ratified by the U.S. Congress in December 1993. The Mexican government sighed with delight. The celebration, however, did not last, as an armed rebel movement appeared in the state of Chiapas on New Year's Day, denouncing both local conditions and the signing of the accords. The rebellion shocked the world. A few weeks later, in March 1994, the official candidate of the national ruling party (PRI), Luis Donaldo Colosio, was assassinated, provoking the most serious political crisis since 1928. A bitter, violent and highly competitive election saw another member of the PRI in the presidential seat. In an effort to stave off speculation, panic, and recession, the government kept the peso artificially high in the wake of the assassination of Colosio. The strategy reached its denouement in December 1994 with the massive collapse of the nation's currency by one-half and triggering a wave of inflation. To check inflation, the new government of Ernesto Zedillo adopted harsh stabilization measures, provoking the worst economic crisis in forty years. The many and sudden developments of 1994 left everyone in the United States wondering if this was the same Mexico they had signed an accord with the previous year. Expectations on both sides plummeted. Mexico was heading toward an immanent moratorium on the short-term payments of its external debt, and had President Clinton not granted the country an emergency loan through executive decision, it was unlikely that the proposal could have gone through Congress. Everyone felt betrayed: Mexicans and their dreams of modernity; Wall Street investment bankers, seduced by technocrats and the lure of easy money; and the U.S. middle classes, who saw their pension monies lost away in a place they could scarcely pronounce.

For U.S. officials, the Mexican crisis was a wake-up call revealing a very deep ignorance of events in that country. Blinders and self-delusions had been too strong. They saw a highly qualified and ambitious group of technocratic reformers rapidly constructing a modern country, previously plagued by corruption, inefficiency, and statism. The "collateral effects" of this process of reform were ignored, as was the increasing concentration of wealth and rising levels of violence. If the stylized image of the country held by bureaucrats and officials was wrong, how would contemporary Mexico be best described? Castañeda offered an answer. It was obvious that U.S. impressions were wrong. Mexico was not a model developing country for others to emulate. It was also not a miracle of modernity. It was, simply, *different*. The Mexican crisis and the ensuing confusion allowed for the resurrection of what could be termed the "theory of difference," a mix of anthropological arguments, literary intuitions, and historical claims about the primordial singularity of Mexico and Mexicanness (*"lo mexicano"*).[30] The events of 1994 made the earlier arguments appear valid once again.

Castañeda stressed the existence of "ferocious differences" between the two countries in an article published by *The Atlantic Monthly*.[31] The principal lesson of 1994 was that whatever similarity Mexico had with the United States was purely coincidental. Mexico could not easily be understood by outsiders, especially Americans. It remained "opaque." "As so often in the past," he exclaimed, "a deeper series of factors made Mexico mysterious, even to the most trained or sympathetic eye. The key to these factors, the single element that explains the opacity of Mexican society and politics to so many, is the simple but critical fact that Mexico is radically, substantively, ferociously different from the United States, and will remain so for the foreseeable future. The mistake that many outside of Mexico made was to believe that the highly perceptible differences of the past were superficial enough to be swept away by a modernizing leader and an apparent acquiescent population."[32] A "deep" Mexico persisted, despite being suppressed by "foreignized" elites.[33] Social differences and endemic violence precluded the "principal indicators" of academics, sages, technocrats of the United States and elsewhere from "operating in Mexico."

This "difference" was so profound, according to Castañeda, that Mexico not only challenged the tools of social scientists but also the experience of "time" itself. Again, the argument was not new, having been first proposed by Octavio Paz in the 1950s. Time, in Mexico, was slower, less imposing; punctuality less important and time was, simply, not money. Since everything was slower, events did not necessarily demand immediate attention. Establishing cause-and-effect relationships was inherently difficult. "Mexican history appears to be one long continuum, with great and long constants and underlying continuities, and only sporadic bursts of compressed, highly-intense events." Inequality, time, and history are essential and enduring differences between the two countries.

Such an emphasis on "difference," found a receptive audience in the United States, in part because the strategy had been tried and proven before. After all, the Japanese managed to disseminate for many years the idea that their society was fundamentally "different" and inaccessible to Western observers. Their customs unintelligible to strangers and their cosmovision even more so. The appeals to incommensurability also served to mask Japanese discrimination against women and other groups and to protect their internal markets against "alien" goods.

The culturalist note also struck an internal nerve within U.S. society. Many of its intellectuals bow their heads before any cultural revindication. On university campuses, diverse ethnic minorities demand symbolic "reparations" for historic wrongs committed against them. These reparations take the form of public acknowledgments of collective injustices of the past and contemporary psychic damage. The corollary to this psychohistorical argument is that all cultures are intrinsically equal and valuable. Everybody has grievances to vent in the United States: Native Americans because of genocidal governmental policies and theft of lands; Afro-Americans because of the legacy of slavery; immigrants and women because of continuing discrimination. The self-esteem of each of these individuals has been diminished by historic wrongs. These feelings, in turn, must be compensated through university instruction of the history and culture of their countries of origins. Somehow this will make the pain go away and instill pride and confidence. Once white America makes a collective apology, a process of healing can begin. Whoever does not recognize the singularity and difference of these groups is a "racist," "sexist," or "intolerant." It has become "bad taste" to call to question many of these aspects of cultural "pluralism."

Castañeda's stress on the constitutive signs of Mexican difference satisfied a latent necessity for coherence by Americans. A. Ruy Sanchez has written about this phenomenon. As the United States becomes ever more diverse as a nation, culturally and ethnically (and less definable as a compact of shared values and characteristics) more Americans wish to see in Mexico a "rigidly defined culture, instead of a complex plurality." Increasingly, more and more Americans project upon Mexico a feeling of unity and solid identity they themselves feel has been lost in their own country.[34] In a sea of existentialist torment, the "Other" is a lighthouse that guides and indicates the proper course. If for Americans it is increasingly difficult to answer the question, Who are we?, at least they know who they *are not*.

The article in *The Atlantic Monthly* touched on another sensitive topic, illegal migration. Castañeda ended his essay on a provocative note, in light of the increasing anti-immigrant feelings in the United States. He wrote, "The United States has traditionally made the right choice between what it considers two connected evils: Mexican instability and Mexican immigration. It fears both but clearly prefers the latter, knowing the former would only worsen matters. Indeed, immigration has not been a problem in binational relations but, rather has been part of the solution to other, graver problems. Some Americans, undoubtedly more than before, dislike immigration, but there is very little they can do about it, and the consequences of trying to stop immigration would certainly be more pernicious than any other conceivable advantage."[35] The claims of inevitability were dubious and more importantly, counterproductive. Little was done in an effort to persuade the doubting and uncommitted, while incitement abounded. It was a slap in the face to those who felt that immigration was a serious issue for the United States and sought to effect policy changes. Between the lines, one could read an apology for a peculiar irresponsibility: the United States was condemned, argued Castañeda, to act as a "safety valve" for Mexico. "Verbiage aside," wrote a reader in response, "Castañeda means that Mexico lost half its territory in the nineteenth-century and will never forgive the United States. . . . Why can't Mexico learn to take advantage of its neighbor's affluence?"[36] Another reader commented that, "Apparently what Mexico really needs is an outright revolution with a few ruling class heads on the pikes to initiate change. This would be far more palatable to many in the United States than the social revolution we will face at home if the gradual Mexican invasion of illegal immigration is allowed to continue."[37] It seems that Castañeda's call for a quiet resignation on the part of the American public on Mexican immigration was unacceptable to many. "I vote for a Mexican Revolution," argued a third reader. "It may solve the immigrant problem in California, because many of *la raza's* militants could return to their homeland and fight for justice in a land in which Mexicans are genuinely oppressed (Mexico), instead of asking for special privileges in a tolerant country that unwisely admitted them (the United States)."[38] The American national spirit was not in a generous mood, judging from the angry letters to the editor.

But, was Castañeda's overall argument solid? Modernity has always obsessed Mexican elites to the point that it has been further subverted in an effort to arrive at its gates quicker. This is precisely what took place in the early nineties, when a facade of progress and modernity was erected upon a very unstable structure that could not hold. While it is true that Mexico is not a member of the advanced industrial nations, it is equally true that "deep" Mexico is itself an intellectual construct more than a lived reality. None can deny that important and numerous differences exist between Mexico and the United States. The border divides more than just neighbors. These differences, however, are not ontological. Most Mexicans, like most of the people of the world, seek a very basic goal: an improved standard of living. This wish burns deep in the hearts of many and accounts for the difficult and often dangerous decision to enter the United States illegally in pursuit of their dreams. The hunger for a decent standard of living, in terms of employment, diet, housing, health, education, and general consumption is stronger than national differences.[39]

The crises of 1994 were not the result of inevitable Mexican "differences." Much of the blame can go to the authoritarian nature of the political system and its handling of the economy. Authoritarianism is not just a Mexican phenomenon, although some observers believe that Mexicans have "perfected" it. Unfortunately, it is an all-too common facet (although highly varied) across the contemporary global landscape. In much the same manner, there is nothing primordial about violence. Violence in Mexico, as in other parts of the world, is the product of specific social, political, and historical conditions that can and should change. Young black males of the southside of Chicago, for example, have comparable rates of life expectancy as males from some of the most economically depressed zones of the Mexican state of Oaxaca. The "opacity" of a nation depends upon the eye of the beholder. Many of the differences that Castañeda alludes to are real, but not decisive or directly relevant in explaining the events of 1994. They also can be comprehended, even by outsiders. Mexico is a complex nation that operates within multiple senses of time. But then again, so does the rest of the world. Clearly, the sense of time is different for a yuppie in Mexico City and a mountaineer in Appalachia or Montana. Yet, links between these "worlds" are often much more subtle and extensive than we imagine. The case of Theodore Kaczynski, the so-called "Unabomber," is a good example of the intersection of these worlds. Kaczynski, a one-time mathematics professor at the University of California-Berkeley, left his job because of a deep sense of malaise and alienation about the effects of technology in the modern world and sought out a minimalist existence in a cabin in the mountains of Montana. He dedicated himself, according to the Federal Bureau of Investigation (FBI), to a rustic life that included doing odds jobs for pay, hunting rabbits, and sending letter bombs to people he felt were contributing to the degradation of this world through their scientific activities. The FBI also claims to have found, in a search of his cabin, letters of correspondence with a sixty-eight-year-old peasant from the Mexican state of Chihuahua named Juan Sanchez Arreola. Apparently, the "Unabomber" was an ardent fan of the Mexican revolutionary Pancho Villa.[40]

The idea of a "deep" Mexico opens an escape hatch away from modernity. Mexican intellectuals have been fascinated with the existence of a rejected, faceless, and silent majority. Deep Mexico cannot be polled. This "imagined country" like all others, has become the carrier of desires, hopes, and fears for those claiming to speak on its behalf. In the forgotten places of Mexico, there is no disenchantment, memory never dies, differences sharpen, and time stands still. Deep Mexico is the last frontier, the last respite where intellectuals can still convincingly substitute civil society.

Although differences exist, this does not imply that the experiences of others are unintelligible. It simply means that understanding others is never easy, always demanding great effort and comprehension. This is equally true for all cultures, which usually share a greater number of similarities than dissimilarities. Mexico is formed by memories and myths. Its true singularity rests not with its historic memories, nor with its shameful inequities. Rather, the singularity rests with the clear conviction of its intellectual elites in Mexico's singularity ("*como México no hay dos*"), a clear and persistently powerful tautology that can be expressed in as many languages as the cosmopolitan nationalists can muster.

The Present of an Illusion: Armed Struggle Instead of Elections

Much of the left at the end of the twentieth century suffers from an accelerated process of (ideological) aging. The Communist utopia lasted seventy years, a brief existence compared to the lifespan of other doctrines. Its dreams of redemption flickered and fascinated like stars in the night. Its history yet to be fully written. For some places, this would amount to entire chapters of national history, while for others a paragraph or simply a line or two. Castañeda pointed to a central paradox in *Utopia Unarmed*: the Latin American left never managed to attain power, except in few and brief moments. Across the board, it was defeated in a war without mercy. Somehow, someway, it managed to persevere in the face or extreme adversity, challenging the doomsayers predictions of complete extinction. Some have argued that the collapse of the Soviet Union did not undermine the Mexican left.[41] The argument is difficult to sustain, for the global faith of a better world through the communist route is shattered. Mexico was not immune to this process of disillusionment.

With the fall of the Berlin Wall, the left turned its gaze to liberalism, asking whether it was sufficiently elastic enough to accommodate the countless number of socialist orphans as well as their aspirations.[42] Was liberalism capable of bringing about a better world? Or was it doomed to act as another ideological disillusion, a liberal utopia?

Utopia Unarmed was originally written in English (later translated to Spanish) and targeted to a large U.S. audience receptive to coverage of the Latin American left.[43] The book was well-received, including a review in the *New York Times*, with its tales of intrigue, heroism, brutality, follies, and all-too frequent defeat of the Latin American left. American interest was due in part to its very own direct involvement in the region. One need only mention Guatemala, Cuba, the Dominican Republic, Nicaragua, and El Salvador to trigger Cold War memories.

In many ways, *Utopia Unarmed* was a very hopeful book. It sought to comfort a demoralized left (both in Latin America and the United States) as well as make it more "respectable" and "middle class." American idealism was a low ebb, suffering from what the political theorist Michael Walzer termed "socially adverse phenomena." The 1980s saw organized labor decline after a series of stinging defeats and the civil rights movements seemed to have run out of steam.[44] Great disorganization prevailed with the dwindling of community involvement, floundering of civic spirit, and declining standards of living for many Americans. The left had no answers to the loss of blue-collar jobs and industries, attacks on the nation's welfare system, and other pressing issues. Immigrants became easy targets in this intemperate environment. And conservative hegemony seemed the norm of the day.

Walzer was right on target with his diagnosis. His hopes for intellectual renewal, however rested not in an internal process of transformation, but in the coming of *external* developments. The left-liberals awaited the appearance of new social movements abroad to connect with and jump start their own reorganization of community life. Waltzer was representative of a current of U.S. intellectuals that refused to resign themselves to despair, felt under siege, and clung to a past that seemed to be slipping through their fingers. Many were prisoners to a new reality they could not master.

At heart, progressive intellectuals hope that conservative hegemony would soon pass, taking away the dark skies and allowing the possibility of hope to shine through. Castañeda's book struck a deep chord among children of the New Deal. However, *Utopia Unarmed* cautioned against waiting for social movements to redeem the intellectual left. He added that in Latin America "it was thought that perhaps a new left could emerge from the popular, pluralistic and proliferating movements, triumphing where others had failed."[45] These "new" movements were actually not so new and "far from being separate from the state, were extensively linked to public policies." "Without an electoral connection and association with political parties," he explained, "oftentimes movements were condemned to wither and die, as the exigencies that gave them birth disappeared."[46] U.S. intellectuals would be wise to heed this lesson from the Latin American cases.

Much of the disarray of U.S. left-liberals is due to the divisive ideological positions adopted over the last twenty years. As part of its militant agenda, the left embraced "minority" issues and abandoned older and broader themes of social justice and the elimination of poverty. Structurally, the U.S. economy was massively reorganized since 1973. Entire industries, such as steel and automotive, declined. Thousands upon thousands of blue-collar and middle management jobs disappeared. The phenomenon known as "stagflation" became all-too familiar for Americans in the late 1970s and early 1980s. In short, the New Deal project seemed exhausted. The ascendancy of the New Right under the presidency of Ronald Reagan (1981-1989) signaled a clear effort to break with the welfare state of Franklin Roosevelt and the racial integrationist policies of Lyndon Johnson's "Great Society." In the face of such changes, liberals seemed unable to both fight for minority rights and for broader national issues.

President Richard Nixon first revealed that blue-collar workers ("hard hats") did not share the liberal militance for ethnic, gay, and lesbian groups. "Hard hats" did not share the same values or agenda of the Democratic Party, which they viewed as "hijacked" and less representative of their interests. The noted British historian Eric Hobsbawm wrote that "to compromise a broader movement with specific claims by minority groups, which are not necessarily their electoral base, is to ask for trouble. This is clearly the case of the United States, where the violent reaction against positive discrimination in favor of specific minorities and the excesses of multiculturalism, is today very powerful."[47] To the outside observer, it seems surprising that left-liberals have not been able to make a recovery, particularly since the leading indicators point to a general decline in the nation's standard of living. This lesson was not lost on important sectors within the Democratic Party, and they have been able to secure a two-term president in the centrist Bill Clinton. However, the intellectual left, according to Walzer, remains adrift.

Despite their lack of political imagination, U.S. left-liberals still nonetheless are able to reflect critically upon the history of failed utopias and their previous celebration for armed struggles. This was evident in the case of Mexico and the appearance of the EZLN in 1994. While many were electrified by the indigenous uprising and its romanticism, the most cautious challenged the idea that violence was the "midwife of history." "Why do so many left intellectuals, or intellectuals generally," asked Michael Walzer in 1995, "succumb to one or another version of authoritarianism? We are not just talking about Stalin and the gulags; the same process of fascination and apology repeats itself over again in small or large scale, in China, Vietnam, Cuba, Nicaragua. . . . And in these last months, I have observed many U.S. leftists trying to believe in *Subcomandante* Marcos, even though they know better than to be seduced by the democratic sounding of the prefix 'sub.'"[48]

The EZLN uprising came as a surprise, for so many had stated that utopia had been disarmed in Latin America. Castañeda affirmed that, in the region, the future of the left lay in the conquest of the ballot boxes, in broader coalitions with popular movements and other forces, but not through the use of arms. The myopia of the U.S. left, obsessed with campus wars but incapable of connecting to broader sectors of society, had its Latin American counterparts. In Mexico, like the United States, fundamental changes were taking place right under the noses of its intellectuals. Some Mexicans not only believed in the efficacy of violence in social transformation but actively organized in an effort to bring out such a movement for over a decade in some of the country's poorest regions. Their efforts were most successful in the state of Chiapas where a sizable and deeply committed indigenous movement appeared. The birth and emergence of the EZLN, the most significant Mexican chapter in the post–Cold War, was entirely missed by Castañeda. In a revised and expanded Spanish version of *Utopia Unarmed,* Castañeda tried to save his argument by arguing that the guerrilla forces of Chiapas, because of their use of the mass media and their very limited military capabilities, *were not really true guerrillas*. The argument was strained, bordering on absurdity. The truly relevant issue of the EZLN uprising was not its limited military capabilities, but the challenge it posed to the thesis about the exhaustion of armed struggle as an option for reform. Since 1994, other guerrilla movements have appeared in Mexico. Ironically, the EZLN has been quite critical of most of them. Like few times before, the rebellion in Chiapas surprised everyone, particularly left intellectuals. How could such a serious observer as Castañeda miss it? The answer is that Mexican intellectuals, like those of the United States, have become distanced from their own societies to such a degree that many obvious things elude them. Utopias, for better or for worse, are never really disarmed. The faith and passion that they inspire are formidable. Stalin understood this well and hence ordered the assassination of Leon Trotsky, who after all, was only an "unarmed prophet."

The critics of Castañeda face many of the same frustrations as those of Carlos Fuentes. Much more than ideological differences, what irks them most is the ability that these two intellectuals have in making themselves heard outside of Mexico. Behind the criticism that both "distort" Mexico in "unidimensional" ways lies a peculiar form of impotence: the inability to present alternative arguments with the same force. And this certainly is not due to the two cosmopolitan intellectuals.

Castañeda is one of the most lucid voices in Latin America. Like others, he seeks to formulate a constructive, purposive, and programmatic alternative to existing social and economic models.[49] Despite appearances, his discourse has changed little in over ten years. The message is still the same: "the United States became our neighbor without anyone asking our opinion in the matter. The obligation to live together and resist their eternal attacks, was imposed upon us by force."[50] Castañeda has revealed himself incapable of seeing very far (beyond historic wrongs) and not very close either (Chiapas).

Today, the left finds itself trapped between the dreams of modernity through social democracy that still lacks a political reality and the weight of the past that has restored the legitimacy of an armed path in search of social justice. The gulf continues to grow between the most "enlightened" and the most "aggrieved." They do not speak the same language: the political discourse of some sounds "prehistoric" to others. Those that opted for direct action, find social democrats aloof and disconnected from reality. Castañeda's cosmopolitan left has accepted once and for all, "bourgeois" democracy and market economics. Many, of varying political stripes, find this position acceptable. Nonetheless in his efforts to present the left as "mainstream," he misses an important sector of Mexican society that demands justice here and now, faces extreme conditions, and cares little for political civilities. The increasing number of spontaneous lynchings in the country reveal that more people are finding popular justice an attractive option. The "deep" left, the EPR guerrilla, threatens to overwhelm its more "civilized" brethren, a possibility that would threaten all. It is clear that the utopia was not disarmed; it merely lay dormant. It has awakened from its sleep and we are once again at a crossroads.

Notes

1. On two occasions, the author tried, unsuccessfully, to arrange an interview with Jorge Castañeda. Like many other Mexican public intellectuals, he is beyond the reach of the average citizen. Intellectuals of both the left and right share busy schedules and a common inaccessibility.

2. Alejandro Toledo and Pilar Jiménez Trejo, "Jorge Castañeda: El intelectual como opositor," in *Creación y poder: Nueve retratos de intelectuales* (Mexico: Joaquín Mortiz, 1994), 189.

3. Castañeda denounced acts of intimidation against him as well as the kidnapping of his personal secretary by presumed government agents.

4. Toledo and Jiménez, *Nueve retratos,* 191.

5. Toledo and Jiménez, *Nueve retratos,* 199.

6. Toledo and Jiménez, *Nueve retratos,* 207.

7. David A. Brading, *Los orígenes de nacionalismo mexicano* (Mexico: ERA, 1980).

8. Benedict Anderson, *Imagined Communities: Reflections on the Origin and Spread of Nationalism* (London: Verso, 1991).

9. Edward Shils, *The Intellectuals and the Powers and Other Essays* (Chicago: Univ. of Chicago Press, 1972).

10. Jorge Castañeda, *La utopía desarmada: Intrigas, dilemas y promesas de la izquierda en América Latina* (Mexico: Joaquín Mortiz, 1993), 122.

11. Robert A. Pastor and Jorge G. Castañeda, *Limits to Friendship. The United States and Mexico* (New York: Alfred A. Knopf, 1988).

12. Jorge G. Castañeda y Robert A. Pastor, *Límites en la amistad: México y Estados Unidos* (Mexico: Joaquín Mortiz/Planeta, 1989).

13. Castañeda y Pastor, *Límites en la amistad,* 22.

14. Castañeda y Pastor, *Límites en la amistad,* 23.

15. Castañeda y Pastor, *Límites en la amistad,* 24-25.

16. Castañeda y Pastor, *Límites en la amistad,* 35.

17. Robert A. Pastor, *Integration with Mexico. Options for U.S. Policy* (New York: Twentieth Century Fund, 1993).

18. Noam Chomsky, "Notes on NAFTA," *The Nation,* 29 March 1993.

19. Jose Ángel Conchello, *EL TLC: Un callejón sin salida* (Mexico: Grijalbo, 1992).

20. Castañeda, *La utopía,* 223.

21. "Hasta la integración económica," *Este País* (April 1991): 4-8.

22. R. Inglehart, M. Basañez, and N. Nevitte, *Convergencia en Norteamérica: Comercio, política y cultura* (Mexico: Siglo XXI, 1994), 198.

23. José Antonio Aguilar Rivera, "La nación de Proteo: nacionalismo y Estado en México al final del siglo XX," *Nexos*, 17 (July 1994): 49-63.

24. *Reforma*, 15 November 1995.

25. Jorge G. Castañeda and Carlos Heredia, "Hacia otro TLC," *Nexos*, 16 (January 1993): 46.

26. Jorge G. Castañeda, "Can NAFTA Change Mexico?," *Foreign Affairs*, 72 (September-October 1993): 66-81.

27. X, pseud., "The Sources of Soviet Conduct," *Foreign Affairs*, 25 (July 1947).

28. *Nexos*, 16 (June 1993): 97-104. *Nexos* petitioned to have the congressional testimony of Castañeda and Aguilar made available and then printed it in its magazine.

29. *Nexos*, 16, 197.

30. Foundational texts on Mexican singularity include Samuel Ramos, *El perfil del hombre y la cultura en México* (Mexico: Imprenta Mundial, 1934); Emilio Uranga, *Análisis del ser mexicano* (Mexico: Porrúa, 1954); Octavio Paz, *El laberinto de la soledad* (Mexico: Cuadernos Americanos, 1954).

31. Jorge G. Castañeda, "Ferocious Differences," *Atlantic Monthly*, no. 276 (July 1995): 68-76.

32. Castañeda, "Ferocious Differences," 70-71.

33. The most recent and popular proponent of the idea of "deep" Mexico was the late anthropologist Guillermo Bonfil. See *México profundo: Una civilización negada* (Mexico: Grijalbo, 1990).

34. Alberto Ruy Sánchez, "Approaches to the Problem of Mexican Identity," in *Identities in North America: The Search for Community,* Robert L. Earle and John D. Wirth, eds. (Stanford: Stanford Univ. Press, 1995), 44.

35. Castañeda, "Ferocious Differences," 76.

36. Anthony J. Dimino, *Atlantic Monthly*, no. 276 (October 1995).

37. Mark Fickes, *Atlantic Monthly*, no. 277 (November 1995).

38. Kenneth Barkin, *Atlantic Monthly,* no. 277 (November 1995).

39. The results of polls, indicating that the majority of Mexicans were in favor of NAFTA, were discarded by Castañeda as irrelevant, as many of those polled did not know the specifics of the agreement. Some felt that it would facilitate their employment opportunities in the United States. While polls are highly imperfect, they do give an indication of popular opinion at any one given moment.

40. James Brooke and David Barboza, "In Letters, Window on Life of the Unabomb Suspect," *New York Times*, 10 April 1996.

41. Jaime Sánchez Susarrey, *El debate político e intelectual en México* (Mexico: Grijalbo, 1993), 68.

42. Ira Katznelson, *Liberalism's Crooked Circle: Letters to Adam Michnik* (Princeton: Princeton Univ. Press, 1996).

43. Jorge G. Castañeda, *Utopia Unarmed: The Latin American Left after the Cold War* (New York: Alfred A. Knopf, 1993).

44. Michael Walzer, "The Political Influence of magazines," Seminar organized by the John F. Kennedy School of Government at Harvard University, 1995.

45. Castañeda, *Utopía desarmada*, 236-238.

46. Castañeda, *Utopía desarmada*, 236-238.

47. Eric Hobsbawm, "La política de la identidad y la izquierda," *Nexos*, 19 (August 1996): 46.

48. Michael Walzer, *Dissent* (Winter 1995): 139-140.

49. Galo Gómez, "Jorge G. Castañeda. Córdoba sigue en el gobierno," *Reforma*, 10 June 1996.

50. Jorge G. Castañeda, "El TLC y las relaciones México-Estados Unidos," in *Compromisos con la nación* (Mexico: Plaza y Janes, 1996), 79.

Conclusion

One and the Same:
Grande and Bravo

"His eyes are staring, his mouth is open, his wings are spread," wrote Walter Benjamin about the Angel of History.

His face is turned toward the past. Where we perceive a chain of events, he sees one single catastrophe which keeps piling wreckage upon wreckage and hurls it in front of his feet. The angel would like to stay, awaken the dead, and make whole what has been smashed. But a storm is blowing from Paradise; it has got caught in his wings with such violence that the angel can no longer close them. This storm irresistibly propels him into the future to which his back is turned, while the pile of debris before him grows skyward. This storm is what we call progress.[1]

Throughout these pages I have attempted to avoid falling into the traps of nostalgia. The idea that the past was always better is the perfect expression of the nostalgic spirit. In contrast, my aim was to perform an exercise of memory. The comparison between the intellectual worlds of Mexico and the United States is not in vain, it is a way to unveil a mirror in which we Mexicans and Americans can see each other and recognize ourselves, by perceiving our similarities and our differences.

Both countries are immersed in a profound process of social deterioration. The United States find itself badly prepared to face the end of a hegemony that has obliged it to interact with the international economy. The cost of greater efficiency in world markets has been the gradual destruction of the social security safety net that Americans once enjoyed. Many jobs have migrated south, where labor is cheaper. The wages of unskilled workers have fallen, along with the income of all but the richest. Violence between the races and social classes has taken the heart of the great cities, and little islands of Third World poverty have made an appearance in a country that once was proudly prosperous. The educational system is in crisis, and the upward

119

mobility promised by the American dream is rapidly falling to shreds. In Mexico, social peace, which was the main justification for a regime that resisted democracy with tooth and nail, disappeared in a single blow. Political institutions, for decades a model of stability in Latin America, suddenly tumbled, and the country entered into a period of turbulence from which it has yet to escape. Endemic poverty and social inequality in Mexico have grown sharper in the last ten years. Insecurity, uncertainty, and fear have come to reside in all parts of the nation.

In both countries, the worst passions have been unleashed, sometimes under the guise of justice: vengeance, envy, pettiness, hate, and mistrust. In Mexico, the justice system is a tragedy; in the United States it is a farce. In view of all of this, neither Mexican nor American intellectuals seem to be equal to the circumstances which amount to nothing less than a crisis of civilization. Shock seems to have us enchained; we are becoming ever more confused commentators on our sad surroundings. In some cases, we devote ourselves solely to expanding upon anecdotes, or putting on shows of verbal acrobatics, that is, when we are not succumbing to the temptation to hurl diatribes, or bottling ourselves up in sterile quarrels. Americans, for their part, devote themselves to waging battles on campus.

One of the consequences of the closer commercial ties that now exist between the countries of North America is the search for common affinities, beyond a purely economic arena. Extending bridges is one of the ways to build a North American community. One of the first phases in the construction of a common identity is the identification of common ideas, which could serve as the moorings for a shared experience. In this sense, Robert L. Earle and John D. Wirth have suggested a common body of ideas and traditions.[2] In their line of reasoning, we can see the opportunities for, as well as the difficulty of, extending bridges in North America.

According to Earle and Wirth, social institutions and practices in the United States, Mexico, and Canada are converging. This would give shape to a liberal inheritance shared by the three nations. The idea, in principle, has historical backing: liberalism is part and parcel of the political baggage in all three countries. However, it is when the authors identify particular institutions of each country as examples of shared core values that we can appreciate how difficult it is to find common threads which go beyond the political situation or the lack of familiarity with intellectual traditions.

Earle and Wirth propose institutions which, supposedly, exemplify the greatest achievements of each nation. For Mexico, this institution would be the governmental program of Solidarity (*Solidaridad*), and for the United States, its university system. Like many other policies created during a particular presidential term of six years, the Solidarity program's days were numbered almost from the moment it was created. More than just a plan for community self-management, as the authors present it, Solidarity was a mechanism that served two main functions: to lend a quite precarious respite to extreme poverty, and to enhance the popularity of the president who created it. The traces of populism could not be disguised even in its best moments. Today, the program of Solidarity has disappeared, together with its creator, former President Salinas. On the other hand, as we have already seen, the American university system is very far from being perfect, or for matter, worthy of emulation. The intellectual deformations produced by a life isolated from society are of such magnitude that scores of critics have come forth to propose reforming American universities. Russell Jacoby has illustrated with great eloquence the pernicious effect of campus life on the mind. If there are any institutions that embody the finest traditions of each country, certainly these are not the ones.

In the shared liberal inheritance, Earle and Wirth identify a tension between the rights of the individual and of the group. This point draws attention away from one of the most surprising phenomena of the end of the century: while the rights of the individual gain more ground every day in Mexican society, which has traditionally been collectivist, in the United States the idea of the individual is losing ground to the community. The society of corporations, Mexico, is becoming a society of individuals, while the society of individuals, the United States, is becoming a society of groups. The roles are slowly beginning to reverse. Intellectually, liberalism in the United States is facing more and more opposition: community-minded critics and classic republicans who favor Machiavelli over Locke. The idea of community has bewitched Americans.[3] Perhaps, because in a postindustrial society the word has lost all real social content; communities have to be invented where there are only joint ventures and anonymous individuals.

Earle and Wirth are echoing a revival of pragmatism inspired by Dewey. The authors see in pragmatism a philosophy that is more friendly to diversity and community. In a somewhat forced manner, they draw parallels between the ideas of the Mexican intellectual Octavio Paz and those of Dewey. Deweyian relativism would seem capable of embracing the different societies of North America. However, it would be a legitimate question if we asked ourselves whether Dewey's ideas are the most appropriate ones for building a continental bridge. Although it is possible that Earle and Wirth were not aware of it, by proposing going back to Dewey as a way to create closer ties with Mexico, they were reliving an almost forgotten chapter in the intellectual relations between the two countries. Today, again, Dewey is proposed as a bridge between the two countries. The possibilities and the objections of the past were the same as today.

Dewey rejected, as we have seen, absolutes, among them timeless truths, such as natural rights. It is understandable that relativism would be an attractive philosophy in the search for community between two such dissimilar societies as Mexico and the United States. Pragmatism would seem to be capable of including a wide variety of values and ways of life without favoring any over the others. This would seem to be the ideal way to achieve peace and fraternity in diversity. Is this true?

If one observes the problems afflicting the two societies, it becomes clear that in both countries what has collapsed are the universal parameters of human togetherness, such as respect for the dignity of people and of life. Shouldn't we, rather than embracing relativism, seek instead to install in both countries common standards that respect the dignity of all people, independent of their language, nationality, culture, or skin color? Common parameters would create common responsibilities and a shared code of conduct across national borders.

Although the institutions and strategies proposed by Earle and Wirth are perhaps not the right ones, the fact is that it is possible to extend bridges between both countries and their intellectual communities. Throughout these pages, we have seen examples of how it can be done. The obstacles, indeed, are formidable. There is not just the language barrier, but also the barriers of parochialism and narrowness of vision which have solidified over the years. Few are willing and able to speak; almost none are willing to listen.

The metaphor of the river that unites/separates the two countries reveals an imaginary line dividing the two worlds that each exist within their respective margins. The river, like Janus, has two faces, one looking to the south, the other to the north. There will again be an intellectual bridge when we recognize that the river is at once *Grande*, and *Bravo*. At the very least, this is a grand and brave idea.

Notes

1. Walter Benjamin, *Illuminations* (New York: Schocken Books, 1969), 257-258.

2. Robert L. Earle and John D. Wirth, "Conclusion: The Search for Community," in *Identities in North America. The Search for Community,* Robert L. Earle and John D. Wirth, eds. (Stanford: Stanford University Press, 1995), 195-225.

3. For example, see: Michael Sandel, "Democrats and Community," *The New Republic*, 22 February 1988.

Bibliography

Aguilar Camín, Hector, and Enrique Krauze. "La saña y el terror." *La cultura en México*, no. 490 (30 June 1971).

Aguilar Rivera, José Antonio. "La Nación de Proteo: Nacionalismo y Estado en México al final del siglo XX." *Nexos* 17, no. 199 (July 1994).

————. "Las razones de la tormenta: violencia y cambio político en México." *Nexos* 19, no. 220 (1996).

Agustín, José. *Tragicomedia Mexicana*. 2 vols. Mexico: Planeta, 1992.

Anderson, Benedict. *Imagined Communities: Reflections on the Origin and Spread of Nationalism*. London: Verso, 1991.

Appleby, J., L. Hunt, and M. Jacob. *Telling the Truth About History*. New York: Norton, 1994.

Arriola, Carlos, comp. *Testimonios sobre el TLC*. Mexico: Porrúa, 1994.

Baer, Delal. "Lo que es ser mexicanólogo." *Reforma* (Mexico), 14 July 1995.

Barber, Benjamin. *An Aristocracy of Everyone: The Politics of Education and the Future of America*. New York: Oxford University Press, 1993.

Barkin, Kenneth. *The Atlantic Monthly*, no. 277 (November 1995).

Barr, Catherine, ed. *The Bowker Annual: Library and Book Trade Almanac*. New Jersey: R. R. Bowker, 1995.

Bartra, Roger. *Oficio mexicano*. Mexico: Grijalbo, 1993.

Bellah, Robert N., et al. *Habits of the Heart, Individualism and Commitment in American Life*. Berkeley: University of California Press, 1985.

Benda, Julien. *The Treason of the Intellectuals*. New York: Norton, 1969.

Benjamin, Walter. *Illuminations*. London: Fontana, 1973.

Bérubé, Michael. *Public Access: Literary Theory and American Cultural Politics*. London: Verso, 1994.

Blanco, José Joaquín. *Se llamaba Vasconcelos: Una evocación crítica*. Mexico: Fondo de Cultura Económica, 1971.

Bloom, Allan. *El cierre de la mente moderna*. Barcelona: Plaza y Janés, 1989.

Bonfil Batalla, Guillermo. *México profundo: Una civilización negada*. Mexico: Grijalbo, 1990.

Bourricaud, François. "The Adventures of Ariel." *Daedalus* 101, no. 3 (summer 1972).

Brading, David A. *Los orígenes del nacionalismo mexicano.* Mexico: ERA, 1980.

Braun, Herbert. "Protests of Engagement: Dignity, False Love, Self-Love in Mexico during 1968." *Comparative Studies in Society and History* 39, no. 3 (July 1997).

Brimelow, Peter. *Alien Nation: Common Sense about America's Immigration Disaster.* New York: Random House, 1995.

Britton, John A. "Moisés Sáenz: Nacionalista mexicano." *Historia Mexicana* 22, no. 1 (July-September 1972).

Bromwich, David. *Politics by Other Means: Higher Education and Group Thinking.* New Haven: Yale University Press, 1992.

Brooke, James, and David Barboza. "In Letters, Window on Life of the Unabomb Suspect." *New York Times,* 10 April 1996.

Brunner, José J. *Educación superior en América Latina: Cambios y desafíos.* Mexico: Fondo de Cultura Económica, 1990.

Camp, Roderic Ai. *Los intelectuales y el Estado en el México del siglo XX.* Mexico: Fondo de Cultura Económica, 1995.

Camp, R. A., C. A. Hale, and J. Zoraida Vázquez, eds. *Los intelectuales y el poder en México.* Mexico: El Colegio de México; Los Angeles: UCLA, 1991.

Carballo, Emmanuel. *Diecinueve protagonistas de la literatura mexicana del siglo XX.* Mexico: Empresas Editoriales, 1965.

Careaga, Gabriel. *Los intelectuales y la política en México.* Mexico: Editorial Extemporáneos, 1971.

"Carlos Fuentes traduce a Nicaragua en Estados Unidos: Ernesto Cardenal." *Proceso,* no. 607 (20 June 1988).

Carson, Tom. "The Long Way Back." *Village Voice* (12 May 1987).

"Carta de Leon Wieseltier." *Proceso,* no. 1009 (4 March 1996).

Castañeda, Jorge G. *La utopía desarmada: Intrigas, dilemas y promesas de la izquierda en América Latina.* Mexico: Joaquín Mortiz, 1993.

————. *Utopia Unarmed: The Latin American Left after the Cold War.* New York: Alfred A. Knopf, 1993.

————. "Can NAFTA Change Mexico?" *Foreign Affairs* 72, no. 4 (September-October 1993).

————. "Ferocious Differences." *The Atlantic Monthly* 276, no. 1 (July 1995).

————. *México-Estados Unidos: Historia de un amor oblícuo.* Mexico: Aguilar, 1996.

Castañeda, Jorge G. and Carlos Heredia. "Hacia otro TLC." *Nexos* 16, no. 181 (January 1993).

Castañeda, Jorge G., and Robert A. Pastor. *Limits to Friendship: The United States and Mexico.* New York: Alfred A. Knopf, 1988.

Castañeda, Jorge G., and Robert A. Pastor. *Límites en la amistad: México y Estados Unidos.* Mexico: Joaquín Mortiz/Planeta, 1989.

Centeno, Miguel Angel. *Democracy Within Reason: Technocratic Revolution in Mexico.* Pennsylvania: Pennsylvania State University Press, 1994.

Chávez Montes, Julio. *Heridas que no cierran.* Mexico: Grijalbo, 1988.

Cherem, Silvia. "Amistades y enemistades." *Reforma* (Mexico), 29 April 1996.

Chomsky, Noam. "Notes on NAFTA." *The Nation* (29 March 1993).

Cockcroft, James D. *Intellectual Precursors of the Mexican Revolution, 1900-1913.* Austin: University of Texas Press, 1976.

————. *Outlaws in the Promised Land: Mexican Immigrant Workers and America's Future*. New York: Grove Press, 1986.

Cohen, Sol, ed. *Education in the United States: A Documentary History 5*. Los Angeles: University of California Press, 1974.

Compromisos con la nación. Mexico: Plaza & Janes, 1996.

Conchello, José Angel. *El TLC: Un callejón sin salida*. Mexico: Grijalbo, 1992.

"Contestación del editor de *The New Republic* a Flores Olea: en Estados Unidos los escritores no cumplen encargos de la Casa Blanca." *Proceso*, no. 1007 (19 February 1996).

Cueli, José. "Carlos Fuentes y la moral literaria." *La Jornada* (Mexico), 3 July 1988.

Damrosch, David. *We Scholars: Changing the Culture of the University*. Cambridge: Harvard University Press, 1995.

De la Concha, Gerardo. *La razón y la afrenta. Antología del panfleto y la polémica en México*. Toluca, Mexico: Instituto Mexiquense de Cultura, 1995.

Delpar, Helen. *The Enormous Vogue of Things Mexican: Cultural Relations beetween the United States and Mexico 1920-1935*. Tuscaloosa: University of Alabama Press, 1992.

Dewey, John. *The Public and Its Problems*. New York: Henry Holt, 1927.

————. *Liberalism and Social Action*. New York: Putnam's, 1938.

————. *Impressions of Soviet Russia and the Revolutionary World, Mexico, China, Turkey, 1929*. Edited by William W. Brickman. New York: Columbia University Press, 1964.

Dimino, Anthony J. *The Atlantic Monthly*, no. 276 (October 1995).

Domínguez, Christopher. *Tiros en el concierto: Literatura mexicana del siglo V.* Mexico: ERA, 1997.

Dorrien, Gary. *The Neoconservative Mind: Politics, Culture and the War of Ideology*. Philadelphia: Temple University Press, 1993.

Earle, Robert L., and John D. Wirth., eds. *Identities in North America. The Search for Community*. Stanford: Stanford University Press, 1995.

Editorial. *Reforma* (Mexico), 15 November 1995.

Editorial. "Hacia la integración económica." *Este País*, no. 1 (April 1991).

Elshtain, Jean-Bethke. *Democracy on Trial*. New York: Basic Books, 1995.

Eyerman, Ron. *Between Culture and Politics: Intellectuals in Modern Society*. Cambridge: Polity, 1994.

Fell, Claude. *José Vasconcelos: Los años del águila (1920-1925)*. Mexico: Universidad Nacional Autónoma de México, 1989.

Fink, L., S. T. Leonard, and D. M. Reid, eds. *Intellectuals and Public Life. Between Radicalism and Reform*. Ithaca: Cornell University Press, 1996.

Flores Olea, Víctor. *Rostros en movimiento*. Mexico: Cal y Arena, 1994.

————. *La espiral sin fin: Ensayo político sobre México actual*. Mexico: Joaquín Mortiz, 1995.

————. "Breve respuesta a un seráfico poeta y a un tartufo historiador." *Proceso*, no. 1006 (12 February 1996).

————. "Krauze o la condición del escritor mercenario." *Proceso*, no. 1008 (26 February 1996).

"Flores Olea entra al debate: Paz, Córdoba y Otto Granados maniobraron para removerme de Conaculta." *Proceso*, no. 1004 (29 January 1996).

Fuentes, Carlos. "Latinos vs. gringos: algunas duras verdades." *Holiday* (October 1962). Cited in *Proceso*, no. 972 (19 June 1995).

————. "¿López Mateos mediador? Dos caminos conducen a la guerra; uno a la paz." *Siempre!* 7 (November 1962).

————. "Opciones críticas en el verano de nuestro descontento." *Plural* 11, no. 2 (August 1972).

————. "Los escritores y la política." *Plural* (13 October 1972).

————. *Latin America At War With the Past.* New York: CBS Enterprises, 1985.

————. *Myself with Others: Selected Essays.* New York: Farrar, Straus & Giroux, 1988.

————. *Nuevo tiempo mexicano.* Mexico: Aguilar, 1994.

————. *La frontera de cristal.* Mexico: Alfaguara, 1995.

————. "Treinta años después." *Proceso*, no. 972 (19 June 1995).

————. "En medio del desplome, la injuria de los crímenes y la corrupción." *Proceso*, no. 997 (11 December 1995).

————. "Retratos en el tiempo." *La Jornada Semanal*, no. 59 (21 April 1996).

Gagnon, Paul. "What Should Children Know?" *The Atlantic Monthly* 276, no. 6(December 1995).

García-Robles, Jorge. *La bala perdida: William S. Burroughs en México (1949-1952).* Mexico: Ediciones del Milenio, 1996.

Gitlin, Todd. *The Sixties: Days of Rage, Days of Hope.* New York: Bantam, 1987.

Godoy, Ricardo. "Franz Boas and his plans for an International School of American Archeology and Ethnology in Mexico." *Journal of the History of the Behavioral Sciences* 13 (1977).

Gómez, Galo. "Jorge G. Castañeda. Córdoba sigue en el gobierno." *Reforma* (Mexico), 10 June 1996.

González Casanova, Pablo. *La democracia en México.* Mexico: Grijalbo, 1965.

González de Alba, Luis. *Los años y los días.* Mexico: ERA, 1975.

Gramsci, Antonio. *La formación de los intelectuales.* Mexico: Grijalbo, 1967.

————. *Selections from the Prison Notebooks.* New York: International Publishers, 1992.

Greenwalt, Kent. *Fighting Words: Individuals, Communities, and Liberties of Speech.* Princeton: Princeton University Press, 1995.

Guerra, François-Xavier. *Modernidad e independencias: Ensayos sobre las revoluciones hispánicas.* Mexico: Fondo de Cultura Económica/Mapfre, 1992.

Guevara Niebla, Gilberto, comp. *La catástrofe silenciosa.* Mexico: Fondo de Cultura Económica, 1992.

Guevara Niebla, Gilberto, and Eduardo Mancera. "El desempeño educativo en América del Norte. Evaluación del aprendizaje en siete grandes ciudades." *Educación 2001*, no. 3 (August 1995).

Guevara Niebla, Gilberto, and Néstor García Canclini, coords. *La educación y la cultura ante el libre comercio.* Mexico: Nexos/Nueva Imagen, 1994.

Gunnel, John G. *The Descent of Political Theory: The Genealogy of an American Vocation.* Chicago: University of Chicago Press, 1993.

Hale, Charles A. "Frank Tennenbaum and the Mexican Revolution." *Hispanic American Historical Review* 75, no. 2 (May 1995).

Harvey, Neil. *Mexico: Dilemmas of Transition.* London: Institute of Latin American Studies, 1993.

Hernández Busto, Ernesto. *Perfil derecho: Siete escritores de entreguerras.* Mexico: Aldus, 1996.

Hernández, Jorge. *Carlos Fuentes: territorios del tiempo.* Mexico: Fondo de Cultura Económica, 1999.

Hiriart, Hugo. "¿Todos contra Krauze?" *La Jornada,* 24 July 1988.

Hobsbawn, Eric. "La política de la identidad y la izquierda." *Nexos* 19, no. 224 (August 1996).

Hofstadter, Richard. *Anti-intellectualism in American Life.* New York: Vintage, 1963.

Hollander, Paul. *Anti-Americanism: Irrational and Rational.* New Brunswick: Transaction, 1995.

Hook, Sidney. *John Dewey: Philosopher of Science and Freedom.* New York: Barnes & Noble, 1950.

Hughes, Robert. *Culture of Complaint: The Fraying of America.* New York: Warner Books, 1994.

Inglehart, R., M. Basáñez, and N. Nevitte. *Convergencia en Norteamérica. Comercio, política y cultura.* Mexico: Siglo XXI, 1994.

Instituto Nacional de Estadística, Geografía e Informática (INEGI). *Estadísticas históricas de México.* Mexico: INEGI, 1994.

Jacoby, Russell. *The Last Intellectuals: American Culture in the Age of Academe.* New York: Noonday Press, 1993.

———. *Dogmatic Wisdom: How the Culture Wars Divert Education and Distract America.* New York: Doubleday, 1994.

Jacoby, Russell, and Naomi Glauberman, eds. *The Bell Curve Debates: History, Documents, Opinions.* New York: Times Books, 1995.

Johnson, Paul. *Intellectuals.* New York: Harper, 1988.

Katznelson, Ira. *Liberalism's Crooked Circle: Letters to Adam Michnik.* Princeton: Princeton University Press, 1996.

Kirn, Walter. "The Editor as Gap Model. The New *New Republic* and the Politics of Pleasure." *The New York Times Magazine,* 13 March 1993.

Krauze, Enrique. "Los intelectuales mexicanos del 1915." *La Cultura en México* (May 1972).

———. "Pasión y contemplación en Vasconcelos I." *Vuelta* 7, no. 78 (May 1983).

———. "Guerrilla Dandy. The Life and Easy Times of Carlos Fuentes." *The New Republic* (27 June 1988).

———. *Textos Heréticos.* Mexico: Grijalbo, 1992.

———. "Jóvenes de ayer." *Siglo 21* (September 1993).

———. "Cuatro preguntas a Flores Olea." *Proceso,* no. 1005 (5 February 1996).

———. "Los intelectuales y el Estado: la engañosa fascinación del poder." *Proceso,* no. 1005 (February 1996).

———. "No le manden Flores." *Proceso,* no. 1009 (4 March 1996).

———. *Mexico: A Biography of Power: a History of Modern Mexico, 1810-1996.* Translated by Hank Heifatz. New York: Harper Collins, 1997.

————. *La historia cuenta.* Mexico: Tusquets, 1998.

————. *Caudillos culturales de la Revolución Mexicana.* Mexico: Tusquets, 1999.

Krauze, Enrique, and Héctor Aguilar Camín. "De los personajes." *La Cultura en México,* no. 548 (August 1972).

Krauze, E., J. Meyer, and C. Reyes. *Historia de la Revolución Mexicana, 1924-1928. La reconstrucción económica.* Mexico: El Colegio de México, 1977.

Kurzweil, Edith, and William Phillips, eds. *Our Country, Our Culture. The Politics of Political Correctness.* Boston: Partisan Review Press, 1994.

Lasch, Christopher. *The True and Only Heaven: Progress and its Critics.* New York: Norton, 1991.

————. *The Revolt of the Elites and the Betrayal of Democracy.* New York: Norton, 1995.

Leiken, Robert S. "Nicaragua's Untold Stories." *The New Republic* (8 October 1984).

Libertad y justicia en las sociedades modernas. Mexico: Porrúa, 1994.

Lind, Michael. *The Next American Nation: The New Nationalism and the Fourth American Revolution.* New York: Free Press, 1995.

————. "The death of intellectual conservatism." *Dissent* (Winter 1995).

Lindau, Juan D. *Los tecnócratas y la élite gobernante mexicana.* Mexico: Joaquín Mortiz, 1992.

Lorey, David E. *The University System and Economic Development in Mexico Since 1929.* Stanford: Stanford University Press, 1993.

Loyo Bravo, Engracia, ed. *La casa del pueblo y el maestro rural mexicano.* Mexico: Secretaría de Educación Pública/Caballito, 1985.

Maclean, I., A. Montefiore, and P. Winch, eds. *The Political Responsibility of Intellectuals.* Cambridge: Cambridge University Press, 1990.

Mansfield, Harvey Jr. "Democracy and the Great Books." *The New Republic* (4 April 1988).

Molina, Alicia. *Antología de textos sobre educación.* Mexico: Fondo de Cultura Económica/CONAFLE, 1981.

Monsiváis, Carlos. "No por mucho madurar amanece mas temprano." *La Cultura en México,* no. 708 (September 1975).

————. "Rectificaciones y relecturas: y sin embargo lo dijo." *Proceso* (9 January 1978).

Mullen, Edward John Jr. "A Study of *Contemporáneos*: A Revista Mexicana de Cultura (1928-1931)." Unpublished Ph.D. diss., Northwestern University, 1968.

"Myth of Revolution, The." *The New Republic* (April 1986).

Orwell, George. *Rebelión en la granja.* Mexico: Promexa, 1987.

Pacheco, Cristina. *Testimonios y conversaciones.* Mexico: Fondo de Cultura Económica, 1984.

"Para el Departamento de Estado, Carlos Fuentes era en 1962 sólo un engañoso escritor a sueldo, 'antiestadunidense y procomunista.'" *Proceso,* no. 972 (19 June 1995).

Pastor, Robert E. *Integration with Mexico. Options for U.S. Policy.* New York: Twentieth Century Fund, 1993.

Paz, Octavio. *El laberinto de la soledad.* Mexico: Cuadernos Americanos, 1954.

————. *Postdata.* Mexico: Siglo XXI, 1970.

————. "Aclaraciones y reiteraciones." *Proceso* (January 1978).

————. "La conjura de los letrados." *Vuelta,* no. 185 (April 1992).

————. *Itinerario.* Mexico: Fondo de Cultura Económica, 1993.

————. *El laberinto de la soledad, Postdata, Vuelta a El laberinto de la soledad.* Mexico: Fondo de Cultura Económica, 1994.

————. "La comedieta de Ponce." *Proceso,* no. 1003 (22 January 1996).

————. "Un Frégoli nativo." *Proceso,* no. 1005 (5 February 1996).

Peretz, Martin. "Cambridge Diarist—Out of Line." *The New Republic* (April 1986).

Poniatowska, Elena. *La noche de Tlatelolco.* Mexico: ERA, 1973.

Pozas Horcasitas, Ricardo. "El pensamiento social francés en la sociología mexicana." *Revista Mexicana de Sociología,* no. 4 (1994).

"Profiles: John Dewey." *Prospects* 13, no. 3 (1983).

Ramos, Samuel. *El perfil del hombre y la cultura en México.* Mexico: Imprenta Mundial, 1934.

"Respuesta de Jorge G. Castañeda y Adolfo Aguilar Zinser" *Nexos* 16, no. 181 (June 1993).

Ricci, David. M. *The Tragedy of Political Science, Politics, Scholarship, and Democracy.* New Haven: Yale University Press, 1984.

Rippy, J., J. Vasconcelos, and G. Stevens. *American Policies Abroad, Mexico.* Chicago: University of Chicago Press, 1928.

————. *The Transformation of American Politics, The New Washington and the Rise of Think Tanks.* New Haven: Yale University Press, 1993.

Rodó, José Enrique. *Obras selectas.* Buenos Aires: El Ateneo, 1964.

Rorty, Richard. "That Old-Time Philosophy." *The New Republic* (4 April 1988).

Rubio, Rosell. "Industria editorial en Europa y México." *El Angel* (January 1996).

Ruíz, Carmen. *Gamio: Arqueología y nación.* San Cristobal, Mexico: Instituto Chiapaneco de Cultura, 1993.

Rutsh, Metchtchild. *Historia de la antropología en México.* Mexico: Universidad Iberoamericana, 1996.

Sáenz, Moisés. *Carapan: Bosquejo de una experiencia.* Lima: n.p., 1936.

Said, Edward W. *Representations of the Intellectual: The 1993 Reith Lecture.* New York: Pantheon Books, 1994.

Sánchez Susarrey, Jaime. *El debate político e intelectual en México.* Mexico: Grijalbo, 1993.

Sánchez, George J. *Becoming Mexican American.* New York: Oxford University Press, 1993.

Schlesinger, Arthur M. *The Disuniting of America: Reflections on a Multicultural Society.* New York: Norton, 1992.

Schumacher, María Esther, comp. *Mitos en las relaciones México-Estados Unidos.* Mexico: Fondo de Cultura Económica/Secretaría de Relaciones Exteriores, 1994.

Semo, Enrique. "El mundo desolado." *Proceso* (25 October 1978).

Sennet, Richard. *The Fall of Public Man.* New York: Norton, 1992.

Sheridan, Guillermo. *Los contemporáneos ayer.* Mexico: Fondo de Cultura Económica, 1993.

————. *México en 1932: La polémica nacionalista.* Mexico: Fondo de Cultura Económica, 1999.

Shils, Edward. *The Intellectuals and the Powers and Other Essays.* Chicago: University of Chicago Press, 1972.

————. *The Academic Ethic.* Chicago: University of Chicago Press, 1984.

Smith, T. V. *The Democratic Way of Life.* Chicago: University of Chicago Press, 1926.

Snyder, Thomas D., ed. *120 Years of American Education: A Statistical Portrait.* Washington: National Center for Educational Statistics, 1993.

Tannenbaum, Frank. *The Labor Movement: Its Conservative Functions and Social Consequences.* New York: G.P. Putnam Sons, 1921.

————. "The Miracle School." *Century Magazine,* no. 106 (August 1923).

————. *Peace by Revolution: An Interpretation of Mexico.* New York: Columbia University Press, 1933.

Taylor, Charles. *Multiculturalism.* Princeton: Princeton University Press, 1994.

Tenorio Trillo, Mauricio. "The Cosmopolitan Mexican Summer, 1920-1949." *Latin American Research Review* 32 (1997): 224-242.

————. "Stereophonic Scientific Modernism: Social Science between Mexico and the United States, 1880-1930." *Journal of American History* 86 (December 1999): 1156-1187.

————. "Contrasting Social Sciences: Mexico and the U.S., 1880s/1940s. Histories of Interactive Moments." Working paper, Centro de Investigación y Docencia Económicas, Mexico, 1994.

————. "South of the Border: Mexico in the American Imagination, 1914-1947/ Mexico en la imaginacion NorteAmericana: 1914-1947" *Latin American Research Review* 32 (summer 1997).

Toledo, Alejandro, and Pilar Jiménez Trejo. *Creación y poder: Nueve retratos de intelectuales.* Mexico: Joaquín Mortiz, 1994.

Uranga, Emilio. *Análisis del ser mexicano.* Mexico: Porrúa, 1954.

Van Delden, Marteen. "The War on the Left in Octavio Paz's *Plural* (1971-1976)." *Annals of Scholarship* 11 (1996).

Vasconcelos, José. "Los cien libros." Gómez Morín Archive. 284:1306. Instituto Tecnologico Autónomo de México. Mexico City, n.d.

Vasconcelos, José, and Manuel Gamio. *Aspects of Mexican Civilization. (Lectures on the Harris Foundation, 1926).* Chicago: Chicago University Press, 1926.

Vaughan, Mary Kay. *Cultural Politics in Revolutionary Teachers, Peasants and Schools in Mexico, 1930-1946.* Tucson: University of Arizona Press, 1997.

Vázquez de Knauth, Josefina. *Nacionalismo y educación en México.* Mexico: El Colegio de México, 1975.

Vázquez, Josefina Zoraida, ed. *La educación en la historia de México.* Mexico: El Colegio de México, 1992.

Velasco, Jesus. "The Influence of Ideas on Policy Realignments: The Neoconservative Case." Ph.D. diss., University of Texas at Austin, 1995.

————. "La perspectiva oblicua: Jorge Castañeda y su visión de Estados Unidos." Unpublished manuscript (1997).

Villoro, Luis. *En México, entre libros: Pensadores del siglo XX.* Mexico: Fondo de Cultura Económica / El Colegio Nacional, 1995.

Waltzer, Michael. In "The Political Influence of Magazines." Seminar organized by the John F. Kennedy School of Government at Harvard University, 1995.

————. *Dissent* (Winter 1995).

Westbrook, Robert B. *John Dewey and American Democracy.* Ithaca: Cornell University Press, 1991.

Williams, Raymond. *Los escritos de Carlos Fuentes.* Mexico: Fondo de Cultura Económica, 1999.

Zaid, Gabriel. *De los libros al poder.* Mexico: Grijalbo, 1988.

————. "Carta a Carlos Fuentes." *Plural,* no. 12 (September 1972).

Zermeño, Sergio. *México: Una democracia utópica: El movimiento estudiantil de 1968.* Mexico: Siglo XXI, 1978.

Index

León, Luis L., 26
Letras Libres, 48
Lewis, Oscar, 44
liberalism, 58; and the Left, 113
liberals, 82; disarray of U.S., 113
Lind, Michael, 50-51
Lippman, Walter, 54

Mailer, Norman, 80-81
Mansfield, Harvey, 66
Marxism, 47
McGovern, George, 77
Mendieta y Nuñez, Lucio, 27
Mendizábal, Miguel Othón de, 26
Mexican intellectuals, 40, 75
Mexican Left, 115
Mexican Revolution, 3, 14, 26, 79.
    See also Tannenbaum, Frank
Mills, C. Wright, xii, 43-44
Monsiváis, Carlos, 42, 45, 51, 59,
    76
Morones, Luis N., 25, 26
multiculturalism, xviii

NAFTA. *See* North American Free
    Trade Agreement
National Autonomous University,
    xii, 7, 15, 27, 42-43, 49, 64-65
National Council for Culture and
    the Arts, 91
National Review, 50
nationalism, 55, 97, 103, 104
newspapers, 53-54
New Left, 44
New Republic, 50, 76, 78, 84-88, 93
New York Review of Books, 49-50
Nexos, 48, 91
Nicaragua, 80, 83-86
Nixon, Richard, 77
North American Free Trade Agree-
    ment, 66, 101-107
nostalgia, xv, 29, 119. *See also*

Lasch, Christopher
Nussbaum, Martha, 40

Orwell, George, 37

Pastor, Robert, 99-101, 105
Paz, Octavio, xi, 48, 58, 61, 75-76,
    88, 91, 121. *See also* Cold War
Peretz, Martin, 50, 85-86. *See also*
    New Republic
Plato, 8
political participation, 54
Porter Anne, Catherine, xi, 3, 26
pragmatism, 16, 17-18. *See also*
    Dewey, John
Prescott, William, xi
professionalization, 38-40, 44, 50
progressive education, 6, 9, 17, 19.
    See also Dewey, John
public sphere, 49; in Mexico, 53,
    56, 61, 93

Ramos, Samuel, 28, 49
Ravitch, Dianne, 63
Reed, Alma, 3
Reed, John, 82
Rivera, Diego, 25-26
Rodó, José Enrique, 19; *Ariel*, 19.
    See also Vasconcelos, José
Rorty, Richard, 40, 66

Sacks, Oliver, 40
Sáenz, Moisés, 5-7, 10, 16-19, 24,
    26-27
Said, Edward, xvi
Salinas de Gortari, Carlos, 91, 97,
    121
Sánchez Susarrey, Jaime, 60
Sandel, Michael, 40
school of action, 6. *See also*
    Dewey, John
science, 9, 18; writers, 40

About the Author

José Antonio Aguilar Rivera teaches political science at the Centro de Investigación y Docencia Económicas in Mexico City. His work on nineteenth-century political theory and history, intellectual relations between Mexico and the United States, and multiculturalism has been published in Spanish and English. He is also author of *En pos de la quimera: reflexiones sobre el experimento constitucional atlántico* (2000) and *Cartas mexicanas de Alexis de Tocqueville* (1999), which was awarded the "Premio de crítica literaria y ensayo político Guillermo Rousset Banda" in 1999. The Spanish version of *The Shadow of Ulysses* was reviewed in major academic and intellectual journals: *Hispanic American Historical Review, Nexos*, and *La Gaceta del Fondo de Cultura Económica* and won the "Alfonso Reyes National Award" in 1998. Aguilar Rivera is widely published, with work appearing in the *Journal of Latin American Studies, Política y Gobierno,* and *Cardozo Law Review.* He has published books with the presses Fondo de Cultura Económica, Cal y Arena, and Miguel Ángel Porrúa. His work spans across several disciplines: intellectual history, political theory, and literature. *The Shadow of Ulysses* aims precisely at that kind of fruitful cross-fertilization. Aguilar Rivera's work partakes from a comparative approach that denies the parochial boundaries of traditional disciplines. He holds a Ph.D. in political science from the University of Chicago and a B.A. in international relations from El Colegio de México and has received several national awards and international fellowships: by the Rockefeller Foundation, the U.S.-Mexico Fund for Culture, and the Fondo Nacional para la Cultura y las Artes (FONCA). He currently writes on politics and culture in magazines and newspapers.